Beyond Access

Beyond Access

The Hidden Inequalities of Digital Learning and How to Bridge Them

Rowan Hart

Mindful Pages

Published in 2025

ISBN: 9789371773003 (PB)
ISBN: 9789371776462 (eBook)

Published by

Mindful Pages
Imprint of Alpha Editions LLC
312 W. 2nd St #1834
Casper, WY 82601, USA

This book was developed using advanced writing tools to support the drafting and ideation process. All content has been thoughtfully curated, refined, and reviewed to ensure quality and relevance.

Content

Introduction
Beyond the Myth of the Digital Native

The glow of a screen has become the defining backdrop of modern childhood. Whether in crowded classrooms or quiet bedrooms, young people tap, swipe, and scroll with apparent ease. Adults watch this fluency with a mixture of envy and relief. If today's students can instinctively navigate apps, games, and devices that often baffle their elders, then surely, the thinking goes, they are prepared for whatever the digital future holds. The notion of the "digital native" has taken deep root in our cultural imagination: the idea that because young people have grown up immersed in technology, they possess an innate expertise that will naturally translate into learning, critical thinking, and opportunity. It is a seductive story, not least because it absolves us—educators, parents, policymakers—of responsibility. If children are digital natives, then our role is merely to provide the tools, stand back, and watch them flourish.

But the reality is far more complicated, and infinitely more consequential. The digital revolution has not bestowed equal gifts upon all who live within its reach. Instead, it has generated two parallel realities. In one, technology genuinely amplifies opportunity: students harness online resources to deepen their knowledge, create new forms of expression, and connect with communities that widen their horizons. In the other, technology becomes a superficial layer, offering entertainment without empowerment, distraction without depth, and exposure without expertise. To mistake the mere presence of devices for genuine empowerment is to ignore the growing inequalities silently shaping classrooms, homes, and societies.

This book begins by dismantling the myth of the digital native because it is not simply inaccurate; it is dangerous. It blinds us to the gaps that matter most. A teenager may juggle social media platforms effortlessly, yet struggle to distinguish reliable information from propaganda. A child may master the mechanics of a new device in minutes, but lack the sustained attention required to complete a challenging task. A classroom filled with laptops may look modern, yet without guidance, structure, and digital literacy, those machines risk becoming little more than expensive notepads or, worse, portals of endless distraction. The belief that exposure equals expertise obscures these truths. It leaves too many young people underprepared and too many adults complacent.

The challenge, then, is not merely to provide access but to look beyond it. Access is the threshold, not the destination. True digital equity requires more than devices and broadband; it demands literacy, guidance, and cultural readiness. It depends on how technology is used, by whom, and under what circumstances. The students who thrive in the digital age are not necessarily those with the newest gadgets, but those who have mentors—teachers, parents, peers—who help them navigate the online world critically and creatively. They are those whose schools see technology not as a silver bullet but as one tool among many, deployed thoughtfully rather than indiscriminately. They are those whose families can afford not only the devices but also the hidden costs—subscription fees, stable connections, private tutors, or simply the quiet space to learn.

Consider the stark contrast. In one household, a teenager learns to code through after-school clubs, guided by a parent who knows how to encourage inquiry while setting boundaries around distraction. In another, a child in the same city uses the same brand of laptop primarily to stream videos, with little adult involvement or scaffolding, in a home where bandwidth is stretched across siblings and bills are barely met. Both children are "digital natives" by the popular definition, yet their digital lives could not be more different. One accumulates skills, confidence, and opportunity; the other risks being left behind, though both appear equally adept at swiping and scrolling.

Such disparities extend far beyond individual households. Across the globe, national governments and school districts have embraced one-to-one device programmes, convinced that placing a laptop or tablet in every student's hands will revolutionise education. Yet evidence repeatedly shows that these initiatives often fail to produce meaningful gains in learning outcomes unless they are accompanied by careful planning, teacher training, and a broader culture of digital literacy. Simply distributing devices can sometimes worsen inequalities, as more advantaged students and schools leverage them for creative exploration, while disadvantaged peers use them mainly for rote exercises or limited test-prep. What looks like progress on the surface often masks a deepening divide beneath.

This book argues that the hidden inequalities of digital learning are as urgent as any challenge facing education today. They are urgent because the digital age is not coming—it is here. To treat technology in schools as an optional extra, a matter of enrichment or convenience, is to misunderstand the extent to which it already mediates how knowledge is produced, circulated, and consumed. They are urgent because the divides are not static. Inequalities do not merely mirror existing social stratifications; they compound them. A child without broadband today is not only cut off from online lessons but also from the habits of digital discernment, the subtle literacies that accumulate through guided use. And they are urgent because the myths we cling to—about digital natives, about the sufficiency of access, about the neutrality of algorithms—threaten to lull us into inaction at the very moment when clarity and courage are most required.

Yet these inequalities are also timeless in their essence. Every technological shift in education, from the printing press to the television, has raised questions about who benefits, who is excluded, and what forms of knowledge are privileged. The digital age is merely the latest—and by far the most powerful—iteration. Technology does not float above society; it is entangled in culture, class, policy, and power. To understand its impact, we must ask: Who controls the infrastructure? Who sets the rules of engagement? Who teaches, and who is left to figure it out alone? These questions echo throughout history, yet they resound with new urgency in a world where algorithms decide what we see, where platforms shape how we think, and where the line between learning and distraction is razor-thin.

The purpose of this book is to make those hidden dynamics visible. Each chapter peels back a layer of the digital experience that is too often taken for granted. We will begin by examining the illusions that surround students' apparent digital fluency, showing why surface comfort with technology can mask profound gaps in competence. We will then confront the inequalities embedded in infrastructure, the costs and conditions that determine whether access empowers or exploits. From there, the book turns to literacy in the age of algorithms, where discernment is as critical as decoding words once was. Teachers' struggles, parents' roles, cultural factors, and policy blind spots all come under scrutiny, revealing how digital divides are shaped not only by technology itself but by the ecosystems in which it is embedded.

The journey culminates in a reframing: from access to agency. The true measure of digital equity is not whether every child has a device but whether every child possesses the confidence, critical capacity, and creative opportunity to use technology meaningfully. This requires rethinking classrooms, empowering teachers and parents, and recognising that human skills—empathy, curiosity, resilience—are not diminished by technology but made all the more necessary.

The questions at the heart of this book are deceptively simple: What does it mean to learn in a digital age? Who benefits, and who is left behind? And most crucially, what can we do to bridge the divides that threaten to define a generation? The answers are neither straightforward nor uniform, but they begin with seeing clearly. Seeing beyond the comforting myths, beyond the assumption that exposure guarantees expertise, beyond the belief that equality of tools equals equality of opportunity.

You, the reader, are invited into this conversation not as a passive observer but as an active participant. Whether you are a parent, teacher, policymaker, or simply someone concerned about the future of learning, your recognition of these hidden gaps is itself a step towards bridging them. The digital age will not wait for us to catch up; its pace is relentless, its influence ubiquitous. But by sharpening our awareness, by questioning assumptions, and by insisting that equity means more than access, we can ensure that technology serves as a ladder, not a barrier.

The promise of this book is sharper recognition. By the time you close its final pages, you will see digital learning differently. You will see the subtle but decisive ways in which inequality is embedded in infrastructure, literacy, culture, and policy. You will recognise that devices and broadband, though necessary, are insufficient. And you will understand that the true task before us is not to raise a generation of digital natives, but to cultivate digital citizens—young people equipped with the fluency, guidance, and agency to thrive in a world where the digital is inseparable from the human.

That task is neither easy nor optional. It is the measure of whether the digital revolution will widen divides or narrow them, whether it will entrench privilege or expand opportunity. And it begins with moving beyond access, toward the hidden realities that shape learning in the twenty-first century.

Chapter 1
The Screen Illusion

Walk into any school corridor today and the scene is unmistakable: teenagers bent over glowing screens, their thumbs moving with astonishing speed, switching from video to message to meme in a rhythm so fluid it seems almost instinctive. To the casual observer, these young people embody the archetype of the digital age: fluent, agile, and seemingly hard-wired for the technologies that bewilder older generations. The myth of the "digital native" thrives in such snapshots, fuelled by the assumption that constant exposure to devices equates to genuine mastery. Yet when one looks beyond the surface, the picture is far more complex—and far less reassuring. What appears to be fluency often masks fragility; what looks like mastery frequently conceals only shallow familiarity. This chapter seeks to unravel that illusion.

The idea of the digital native has had remarkable staying power since it was first coined at the turn of the millennium. The story was seductive in its simplicity: a new generation, born into a world of laptops, smartphones, and social media, had developed not just comfort with these tools but an innate capacity to harness them for learning and growth. Older generations were cast as "digital immigrants," doomed to struggle with accents and awkwardness in a language that came naturally to their children. The metaphor gained traction in classrooms and policy documents alike, influencing everything from curriculum design to national technology rollouts. Yet metaphors, however powerful, are not the same as evidence. Over two decades later, research consistently shows that exposure does not translate to expertise. Indeed, it often entrenches new forms of inequality, with some students using technology as a genuine springboard for opportunity while others are caught in cycles of superficial use, distraction, or even disempowerment.

Consider the experience of a student in Madrid who navigates social media with aplomb, creating a flawless TikTok video in minutes, syncing music, edits, and captions with precision. She appears digitally skilled, even enviably so. Yet in the same classroom, when asked to evaluate the credibility of two online articles presenting conflicting data on climate change, she struggles. She cites the one with the more polished layout, never questioning its sources or motives. This disjunction between apparent fluency and deeper literacy is the essence of the digital native fallacy. Knowing how to consume, produce, and share content in familiar formats does not mean knowing how to interrogate, synthesise, or apply information. Entertainment literacy is not the same as critical literacy.

The consequences of mistaking one for the other are profound. Across the globe, governments and school systems have poured vast sums into one-to-one device programmes, promising to narrow divides and modernise education. The logic seems unimpeachable: if every student has a device, then every student has equal access to digital opportunity. Yet large-scale evaluations—from the United States' "One Laptop per Child" initiatives to European rollouts and experiments across Latin America—tell a sobering story. Devices without structured guidance often yield little improvement in academic outcomes. In some cases, they even exacerbate inequalities, with wealthier students receiving the scaffolding and encouragement to use devices for exploration and creation, while their less advantaged peers are left with machines that become portals to distraction or tools for basic drill-and-practice exercises. The screen, intended as a leveller, often ends up amplifying divides.

Part of the problem lies in conflating comfort with competence. It is true that many young people move through digital environments with ease, downloading apps, customising profiles, and mastering new platforms in days. Yet such ease is often mistaken for genuine capacity to use technology in ways that enhance learning, problem-solving, or long-term opportunity building. Comfort describes familiarity, a fluency with interfaces; competence demands discernment, intentionality, and transferability of skills. The student who can set up a group chat effortlessly may still falter when asked to structure a research project, filter through competing online claims, or apply a digital tool to a novel context. The gap between comfort and competence is where much of today's educational inequality resides. Those with adult mentors, guided curricula, or access to enrichment programmes often make the leap. Those without are left circling the surface, appearing adept while lacking the depth required to thrive.

Why, then, does the myth of the digital native persist so powerfully? One reason is cultural convenience. For parents and educators overwhelmed by rapid technological change, it is reassuring to believe that young people are naturally equipped to handle it. To imagine otherwise would mean acknowledging uncomfortable gaps and responsibilities. Another reason lies in commercial interest. Technology companies have a vested stake in perpetuating the idea that devices themselves empower, that more screens in classrooms equate to progress. The myth creates markets, fuels demand, and shifts accountability away from pedagogy and towards products. Policy, too, has played a role. Faced with pressure to modernise, governments have often embraced metrics that are easy to count—devices distributed, bandwidth extended—rather than those that are harder to measure, such as the cultivation of critical thinking or the fostering of digital discernment. Exposure is simple to quantify; expertise is not.

Real-world examples underscore these dynamics. In Uruguay, one of the earliest adopters of a nationwide one-to-one laptop initiative, evaluations found that while students became adept at basic computer functions, there was little measurable improvement in learning outcomes unless teachers were extensively trained to integrate the devices into lessons meaningfully. In the United States, districts that invested heavily in tablets often found that without adequate professional development, teachers defaulted to using them as electronic worksheets rather than tools for creativity or collaboration. Meanwhile, in parts of rural India, where bandwidth remains patchy, students given devices often used them primarily for offline games, a reminder that without connectivity and contextual guidance, devices do little to bridge learning divides. Across contexts, the same lesson emerges: screens alone do not transform education. What matters is how they are embedded into ecosystems of teaching, guidance, and cultural readiness.

The illusion persists not only because it is comfortable but because it aligns with longstanding narratives about generational change. Every generation has looked upon the habits of the young with a mixture of wonder and alarm, from the rise of radio to television to video games. The difference now is scale. Digital technologies are not one medium among many; they mediate virtually all aspects of learning, communication, and participation. To mistake surface fluency for depth is to risk building education systems on foundations of sand. The screen illusion—the belief that more devices automatically mean more learning, that comfort equals competence, that exposure ensures expertise—is among the most dangerous assumptions shaping our time. It leads to misplaced investments, unmet expectations, and most damagingly, widening inequalities disguised as progress.

This chapter invites readers to interrogate those assumptions. We will explore why the notion of the digital native is misleading, drawing on case studies that reveal how tech-savvy appearances can hide shallow skill sets. We will examine the evidence around one-to-one device programmes, asking why distributing laptops and tablets so often fails to yield the promised gains. We will unpack the distinction between comfort and competence, recognising that the ability to navigate interfaces is not the same as the ability to apply them meaningfully to learning. And we will trace the cultural, commercial, and policy forces that keep the myth alive, despite mounting evidence to the contrary. In doing so, the goal is not to dismiss the digital generation but to see it more clearly. The young are not digital natives in the sense the myth suggests; they are digital citizens in the making, in need of guidance, scaffolding, and discernment. To believe otherwise is to let the glow of the screen blind us to the realities within.

This is the screen illusion: the dazzling surface that convinces us all is well, even as deeper inequalities grow unchecked. By peeling it back, we begin not with cynicism but with clarity. For only in seeing the illusion for what it is can we begin the more urgent task of ensuring that technology in education serves as an amplifier of opportunity, rather than an architect of division.

The Digital Native Fallacy

Few ideas in contemporary education have proved as persistent or as misleading as the notion of the "digital native." The phrase suggests a generational divide so stark that it seems almost biological: young people, by virtue of being born into a world saturated with devices, are assumed to possess an innate digital fluency, while older generations are cast as perpetual outsiders, destined to fumble awkwardly with every new platform. The metaphor is powerful, but it is also profoundly flawed. It offers a comforting illusion at a time when the realities of digital learning demand far more precision and nuance. *Exposure does not equal expertise, and familiarity does not guarantee literacy.* Mistaking one for the other has shaped education policy, corporate marketing, and parental assumptions for two decades, leaving us dangerously ill-prepared to address the real divides that determine who thrives in the digital age.

The appeal of the digital native myth is obvious. It suggests that a generation raised on touchscreens and search engines has absorbed their logic instinctively, requiring little guidance to make the most of what technology can offer. A child who can master a gaming interface in hours or produce a seamless TikTok video in minutes seems to embody this premise. Yet these examples reveal only a narrow spectrum of skills: navigation, adaptation, and the rapid acquisition of platform-specific mechanics. They say little about the capacities that education and society most require: the ability to distinguish credible from misleading information, to evaluate sources, to structure knowledge critically, and to apply digital tools in ways that build opportunity rather than erode attention. What is often described as fluency is, on closer inspection, more akin to accent—a knack for moving comfortably within certain spaces, but without the grammar and vocabulary necessary for genuine understanding.

Research consistently exposes the gap between perception and reality. A study by the Organisation for Economic Co-operation and Development (OECD) found that students who reported high levels of screen use at school actually scored lower in reading and maths than peers who used digital tools more sparingly but under structured guidance. Similarly, investigations into one-to-one laptop programmes across North America and Europe reveal that the distribution of devices rarely translates into improved outcomes unless accompanied by intensive teacher training and deliberate integration into pedagogy. When devices are left to stand on their own, they too often reinforce existing inequalities: students from more advantaged households, who benefit from parental support and supplemental resources, harness them productively, while those without such scaffolding are left with a tool that offers entertainment but little genuine empowerment.

Consider a widely cited case in Peru, where a national initiative distributed hundreds of thousands of laptops to rural schools under the assumption that access itself would transform learning. Evaluations later showed minimal impact on literacy and numeracy. Students became adept at basic functions—typing, drawing, and offline games—but showed little evidence of improved comprehension or problem-solving. The illusion of empowerment concealed a troubling truth: technology without literacy, guidance, and context risks becoming a hollow gesture, one that promises equality while delivering stagnation. Similarly, in the United States, districts that invested heavily in tablets often found them underused, or used primarily for test preparation rather than creative exploration, thereby reinforcing narrow measures of success rather than expanding horizons.

The persistence of the digital native myth is not merely a matter of misunderstanding; it is actively sustained by cultural, political, and economic forces. For parents anxious about their own unfamiliarity with new tools, it is reassuring to imagine that their children are naturally ahead. For educators under pressure to integrate technology into curricula, the myth suggests less need for intensive retraining or support. For technology companies, it is a marketing boon: if young people are instinctively fluent, then every new device or app can be presented as an opportunity waiting to be unlocked, rather than a tool requiring careful cultivation. Policymakers, too, are drawn to the simplicity of the narrative. Counting devices distributed, or reporting broadband penetration rates, offers a neat, quantifiable metric of progress that looks impressive in reports and speeches, even as the deeper questions of literacy and equity go unaddressed. *The myth endures because it serves too many interests to be easily discarded.*

Yet the evidence of its inadequacy is everywhere. University professors often note that students who are highly proficient with social media arrive unable to manage basic file systems, format documents consistently, or conduct reliable academic searches beyond typing a few words into Google. Employers report similar frustrations: new graduates may appear confident with digital tools but falter when required to use them for sustained problem-solving, collaborative work, or critical analysis. In a study conducted at Stanford University, over 80 per cent of students tested failed to distinguish between sponsored content and legitimate news articles when browsing online. These are not trivial gaps. They reveal a generation that is adept at moving quickly through digital environments but not necessarily skilled at navigating them wisely. *Surface confidence masks underlying fragility.*

It is important, however, to resist caricature. Young people are not incapable, nor are they helpless; they are learners, like any other generation before them, shaped by the contexts in which they are taught and guided. To call them digital natives is to strip away the role of cultivation and mentorship, to pretend that literacy emerges spontaneously without the painstaking scaffolding that has always underpinned true education. Literacy in the print era was never assumed to blossom from exposure to books alone; it required teachers, families, and institutions to nurture comprehension, analysis, and interpretation. Digital literacy is no different. Yet the myth of innate fluency blinds us to this continuity, leaving too many children adrift in a sea of information without the compass of discernment.

The digital native fallacy also obscures the profound inequalities within the generation it supposedly describes. Not all young people grow up surrounded by devices of equal quality, with reliable broadband, or with adults who can guide them through the complexities of digital life. A student in an affluent household may experiment with coding classes, online collaboration tools, or digital art platforms, while a peer in a low-income household may use the same smartphone almost exclusively for messaging and video consumption. Both are labelled digital natives, yet their trajectories could not be more different. The myth erases these distinctions, flattening diversity into a single, misleading category that conceals as much as it reveals.

What emerges from these insights is a need to reframe how we understand digital engagement. Rather than assuming innate capacity, we must recognise a continuum: from surface comfort to genuine competence, from entertainment literacy to critical literacy, from exposure to agency. The first steps on this continuum may come easily—navigation, consumption, adaptation—but the higher-order capacities require deliberate investment. They demand pedagogical shifts, teacher training, parental involvement, and cultural recognition that digital fluency is not inherited but cultivated. Without such investment, the screen becomes less a bridge than a barrier, creating a generation that appears equipped for the future but lacks the deeper skills to shape it meaningfully.

The fallacy of the digital native is not a harmless misconception. It shapes the decisions of parents who outsource responsibility to devices, of schools that conflate hardware with pedagogy, of policymakers who equate connectivity with equity. It allows commercial agendas to masquerade as educational progress, while leaving the most vulnerable students at risk of falling further behind. To dismantle this myth is not to diminish young people's creativity or adaptability, but to insist on a more honest and demanding account of what true digital literacy entails. *Comfort with tools must never be mistaken for competence with ideas.*

By peeling back the illusion, what comes into view is not a generation that is failing, but a generation that is being failed—failed by narratives that obscure their real needs, by policies that measure the wrong things, and by adults who mistake their facility with games and apps for evidence of mastery. The task ahead is not to lament this reality but to correct it, by recognising that digital fluency is neither automatic nor evenly distributed. It is the product of guidance, opportunity, and sustained practice. Only by moving beyond the myth of the digital native can we begin to build systems that prepare young people not merely to consume, but to create; not merely to navigate, but to discern; not merely to live in the digital age, but to shape it with agency and confidence.

When More Devices Don't Mean More Learning

The sight of classrooms filled with laptops and tablets has become a global symbol of progress, a shorthand for modernisation in education. Photographs of smiling students holding their new devices appear in government reports, press releases, and technology marketing campaigns, carrying the implicit promise that the distribution of hardware is synonymous with the distribution of opportunity. Yet the assumption that placing a screen in every child's hands automatically translates into deeper learning has been repeatedly challenged by evidence. *The uncomfortable truth is that technology, without structure, guidance, and context, rarely transforms education; more often, it mirrors and sometimes magnifies the inequalities already present.*

The enthusiasm for one-to-one device programmes—initiatives that aim to provide every student with a laptop or tablet—emerged in the early 2000s, with projects such as One Laptop per Child (OLPC) capturing global attention. The vision was radical: lightweight, durable, low-cost devices would democratise learning across the globe, enabling children in under-resourced regions to leapfrog traditional barriers and join the digital age. Governments and philanthropic organisations embraced the idea, investing billions of dollars into scaling such initiatives. Yet as these devices were rolled out across Latin America, Africa, Asia, and the developed West, a sobering pattern emerged. The physical presence of devices did not, on its own, produce the cognitive, social, or educational outcomes that had been promised. Instead, results were mixed, often disappointingly so.

Evaluations of OLPC in countries such as Peru and Uruguay revealed stark limitations. In Peru, where hundreds of thousands of laptops were distributed to rural students, assessments found little to no impact on mathematics and reading performance. Children learned how to operate the devices, exploring pre-installed programmes and playing games, but there was scant evidence of deeper literacy or numeracy gains. In Uruguay, the programme achieved near-universal coverage, making the country a poster child for digital access. Yet follow-up studies showed that while the initiative succeeded in narrowing the device ownership gap, its effects on learning outcomes were minimal without parallel investments in teacher training and curricular adaptation. Devices were often underused in classrooms, with many teachers defaulting to traditional methods or using laptops primarily for word processing and test preparation.

Similar patterns appear in wealthier contexts. In the United States, districts that pursued ambitious one-to-one tablet rollouts often encountered setbacks when the devices became more source of distraction than of instruction. In Los Angeles, a $1.3 billion initiative to provide iPads to every student collapsed under the weight of poor planning, limited teacher preparation, and software that proved inadequate for instructional needs. In Europe, studies of laptop initiatives in countries such as Portugal similarly highlighted that without strong pedagogical integration, devices were more effective in changing appearances than outcomes. They signalled progress but did not reliably deliver it. *The promise of transformation was undercut by the reality that learning requires more than access to tools; it requires structured use, intentional design, and the human infrastructure to make those tools meaningful.*

Why do so many device-centred programmes fail to achieve their intended impact? Part of the answer lies in the enduring belief that technology is inherently transformative. Policymakers and administrators, under pressure to modernise schools, often mistake the distribution of hardware for educational reform itself. Counting the number of laptops distributed or measuring student-to-device ratios provides easy metrics of progress, while the more complex work of teacher development, curriculum redesign, and cultural adaptation is harder to quantify and less photogenic. In effect, devices are treated as educational ends in themselves rather than as tools whose impact depends entirely on how they are used.

Another reason lies in the practical challenges of implementation. Teachers frequently receive insufficient training to integrate technology meaningfully into their practice. Professional development, when it is offered, often focuses on the mechanics of operating devices rather than on redesigning pedagogy to exploit their potential. Without support, teachers may simply replicate analogue practices on digital platforms, turning laptops into glorified notebooks rather than portals to collaboration, creativity, and critical inquiry. Students, meanwhile, may gravitate toward entertainment or distraction in the absence of structured guidance, especially when devices are taken home without expectations for purposeful use. *The screen may be present, but the learning is absent.*

There are also deeper structural factors at play. The success of one-to-one programmes often depends on conditions beyond the classroom. Reliable internet access, maintenance, and technical support are critical, yet frequently overlooked. In rural or low-income contexts, bandwidth constraints mean that students with devices may still be cut off from interactive resources or collaborative opportunities, leaving them to rely on offline functions that limit the educational potential of the tools. The hidden costs of sustaining programmes—software licences, replacements, technical staff—can also strain budgets, leading to underfunded, short-lived initiatives that fizzle after initial fanfare. Devices alone cannot compensate for inadequate infrastructure or systemic inequities; in fact, they can highlight them, making disparities more visible.

This is not to say that one-to-one device programmes are doomed to fail. There are examples where they have contributed meaningfully to educational outcomes, but the common thread in those successes is that devices were embedded within a broader ecosystem of support. In Singapore, for instance, technology integration has been coupled with substantial investment in teacher training, iterative curriculum design, and sustained evaluation. Rather than treating laptops as panaceas, the system positioned them as one component within a carefully calibrated strategy for cultivating digital literacy and critical thinking. Similarly, some schools in Scandinavia have managed to harness one-to-one programmes effectively by combining them with project-based learning, collaborative tasks, and strong professional communities of teachers who continually refine their practice. In these contexts, the devices are not seen as magic bullets but as instruments requiring orchestration.

The philosophical mistake underlying many failed programmes is the assumption that access alone equals equity. A laptop on every desk may create the appearance of equality, but it does not erase the unequal capacity to benefit from that laptop. Students with supportive families, private tutors, or digital enrichment opportunities outside school are far more likely to use devices for exploration, creation, and skill-building. Their less advantaged peers may be left with narrower uses, sometimes even reinforcing the test-oriented approaches that constrain learning. *What looks equal on the surface can, in practice, deepen divides.*

There is also a cultural dimension to consider. The adoption of technology is shaped not just by infrastructure and training but by beliefs about what learning is and how it should happen. In some contexts, where education is seen primarily as the transmission of fixed knowledge, devices are used to digitise traditional tasks rather than to reimagine them. Worksheets become PDF files, lectures become videos, but the fundamental pedagogy remains unchanged. The potential of technology to foster inquiry, creativity, and collaboration remains untapped. In contrast, when educators embrace more constructivist approaches—seeing learning as an active, student-centred process—devices can become powerful enablers of experimentation and critical thinking. The device itself does not dictate the outcome; the culture around learning does.

The global evidence, therefore, points to a clear but challenging insight: *devices matter far less than what surrounds them.* They can expand opportunity when embedded in ecosystems of training, curriculum, and cultural readiness, but without these conditions, they risk becoming expensive symbols of modernity rather than engines of learning. The allure of the device-centred solution lies in its simplicity, but genuine progress requires grappling with the complexity of education as a human endeavour. To believe that screens alone can carry the weight of transformation is to mistake the medium for the message, the tool for the teaching.

The lesson to draw is neither uncritical enthusiasm nor blanket scepticism, but a demand for discernment. Distributing devices may be necessary, but it is never sufficient. For technology to serve as an amplifier of opportunity rather than a mirror of inequality, it must be embedded in thoughtful pedagogy, robust support, and a recognition that the human infrastructure of learning—teachers, families, communities—cannot be bypassed. *The question is not how many devices students have, but how those devices are woven into the fabric of learning in ways that cultivate competence, confidence, and critical capacity.*

Anything less risks perpetuating the illusion of progress while leaving the deeper problems untouched.

The Comfort vs. Competence Divide

A teenager scrolling through multiple apps, toggling effortlessly between video clips, music playlists, and chat threads, appears remarkably fluent in the digital world. Observers often mistake this ease for mastery, presuming that such dexterity naturally extends to learning, problem-solving, and the capacity to harness technology for opportunity. Yet this assumption collapses under scrutiny. *Comfort with technology is not the same as competence in using it meaningfully.* This distinction—often overlooked in public discourse and policy design—has become one of the most critical dividing lines in education and society, determining who leverages digital tools to advance and who remains stuck at the level of surface familiarity.

Comfort reflects familiarity: the ease with which a person navigates platforms, personalises settings, and adapts to new applications. It is a form of social confidence, reinforced through frequent exposure, habit, and play. Competence, by contrast, demands intentionality: the ability to apply technology purposefully to tasks that require critical thought, sustained effort, and adaptability. Competence is not about how quickly one can post an image to Instagram but about knowing how to evaluate competing sources of information for reliability, how to manipulate a spreadsheet to reveal patterns in data, or how to use a presentation tool not merely to decorate slides but to communicate ideas persuasively. This divide has profound consequences, particularly in education, where the assumption that comfort equals competence has led to misguided strategies, wasted resources, and the quiet reproduction of inequality.

A useful parallel can be drawn with language learning. A child raised in a bilingual household may feel comfortable switching between tongues in casual conversation, but this does not automatically translate into competence in formal writing, grammar, or literature. Similarly, students who have grown up immersed in digital devices often possess intuitive ease with interfaces, but their deeper literacy—the capacity to think critically with and through digital tools—requires explicit cultivation. In many classrooms, this gap plays out starkly. Teachers encounter students who can produce polished videos or memes yet falter when asked to construct a coherent essay using digital resources. The discrepancy lies not in intelligence but in the absence of guided practice that transforms familiarity into capability.

Evidence supports this distinction. A 2018 Stanford study on civic online reasoning revealed that the majority of high school and university students tested could not effectively distinguish between news articles and sponsored content, despite their confidence in navigating digital media. The problem was not access, nor even comfort with platforms, but the absence of critical evaluation skills—a dimension of competence that does not emerge spontaneously from screen time. Likewise, the OECD's research into digital learning environments found that students in countries with high device usage in classrooms did not outperform their peers in traditional settings unless teachers deliberately integrated technology into structured tasks that demanded analysis, collaboration, or creation. Simply being at ease with screens did little to guarantee learning gains; competence emerged only when technology was used with purpose.

The comfort–competence divide also explains why one-to-one device programmes often fall short of expectations. Students may embrace their new laptops with enthusiasm, customising backgrounds, downloading apps, and exploring features. Yet without training in how to use those devices for academic or problem-solving purposes, the novelty often fades into distraction. Competence requires scaffolding: instruction in how to conduct effective online searches, how to organise digital notes, how to evaluate algorithms that shape what information appears first. Without such scaffolding, devices become more tool for leisure than for learning. The result is a generation that appears digitally fluent on the surface but remains underprepared for the demands of higher education and the workplace.

This divide does not affect all students equally. Those from wealthier households often receive additional guidance, whether from parents who are themselves digitally literate or through supplementary programmes that teach coding, digital storytelling, or research skills. Their comfort is more likely to be converted into competence because adults in their lives provide context, discipline, and opportunity. By contrast, students in less advantaged settings may be left to navigate technology alone. For them, devices serve primarily as entertainment or as basic conduits for assignments, with little exposure to higher-order uses that build transferable skills. *The very same devices, then, reinforce rather than diminish inequality, depending on whether comfort is supported and translated into competence.*

Case studies illustrate this divide vividly. In Estonia, often hailed as one of the world's most digitally advanced nations, educational authorities invested heavily not only in devices but in systematic digital literacy curricula, ensuring that students learn from early years how to evaluate sources, protect their privacy, and use tools for creation and problem-solving. Here, comfort and competence are deliberately connected, with tangible outcomes in both academic performance and civic engagement. Contrast this with many large-scale device rollouts in parts of Latin America or sub-Saharan Africa, where laptops were distributed widely but without sufficient teacher training or curriculum adaptation. Students grew comfortable with basic use but gained little competence in applying technology beyond rote or recreational purposes. These differences underscore the reality that competence does not emerge automatically; it must be cultivated through thoughtful design.

One of the most insidious consequences of conflating comfort with competence is the way it shapes adult perceptions. Parents, reassured by their children's apparent dexterity, may assume that no further guidance is necessary. Teachers, intimidated by students' ease with platforms, may underplay their own role in fostering deeper skills. Policymakers, eager to showcase modernisation, may measure success in terms of devices distributed rather than skills developed. The result is complacency: the illusion that young people are prepared when, in reality, many are navigating a complex digital environment with only superficial tools. *The belief that comfort equals competence blinds adults to their continuing responsibility as mentors and guides.*

At the philosophical level, the comfort–competence divide forces us to reconsider what it means to be literate in a digital society. Literacy has never been merely the ability to decode words on a page; it has always involved comprehension, interpretation, and application. In the same way, digital literacy is not the ability to open apps or send messages but the capacity to use digital tools critically, responsibly, and creatively. It involves habits of inquiry, resilience in problem-solving, and ethical discernment in a world where information is abundant but not always reliable. Comfort may be instinctive; competence must be earned.

The divide also raises uncomfortable questions about the future of work. Employers increasingly expect graduates not only to use digital tools but to adapt them for innovation, to collaborate across platforms, and to exercise judgement in contexts shaped by data and algorithms. Yet surveys reveal that many young employees arrive lacking these skills. They are confident with technology but unprepared to deploy it strategically. This gap translates into lost opportunities, both for individuals who struggle to advance and for economies that fail to harness the full potential of a digitally connected workforce. The consequences are long-term, shaping trajectories of social mobility and widening divides between those who can use technology to open doors and those for whom it remains a closed loop of entertainment.

Bridging the comfort–competence divide requires more than technical training; it demands a cultural shift. Schools must stop assuming that students arrive digitally prepared and instead treat digital competence as a core subject, taught and assessed with the same seriousness as literacy and numeracy. Teachers need sustained professional development to integrate digital tools into lessons in ways that require critical application rather than superficial engagement. Families must recognise that guidance extends beyond screen time limits to include coaching in discernment, creativity, and responsibility. And societies must acknowledge that genuine digital equity is not achieved by distributing devices but by ensuring that all young people have the support to move from comfort into competence.

The comfort–competence divide is not a marginal issue; it is a defining feature of how inequality is evolving in the digital age. To ignore it is to accept a world where some students transform their familiarity with devices into platforms for advancement while others remain trapped at the level of passive consumption. To address it is to recognise that competence is the true currency of digital learning, the measure by which education must be judged. Comfort may impress at a glance, but it is competence that determines who thrives, who leads, and who is left behind.

Why the Myth Persists

Few misconceptions in education have proved as enduring—or as damaging—as the belief that growing up surrounded by digital technology automatically produces expertise. The image of the "digital native" retains a powerful hold on cultural imagination, despite repeated evidence that it is little more than a comforting illusion. The persistence of this myth is not accidental. It has been reinforced by a confluence of cultural narratives, institutional practices, and economic incentives that together perpetuate the assumption that exposure equals expertise. To dismantle the myth, it is essential first to understand why so many stakeholders—from parents to policymakers to technology companies—have found it convenient to keep it alive.

At the cultural level, the myth offers reassurance in the face of rapid technological change. Parents who feel outpaced by their children's facility with devices often adopt the narrative of digital nativeness as a psychological defence. The idea that their child is naturally equipped for the digital age reduces anxiety about their own lack of literacy. A parent who struggles with cloud storage or online banking may interpret a teenager's ability to set up a new smartphone or navigate social media as evidence that the younger generation requires no guidance. In reality, what is being observed is surface comfort rather than deeper competence, but the myth provides a convenient alibi: if children are self-sufficient in digital spaces, parents are relieved of the pressure to mentor them there. *Believing in the myth allows adults to abdicate responsibility without guilt.*

Educators, too, can fall prey to similar reasoning. Faced with classrooms full of students who appear at ease with apps and devices, teachers may assume that their role is limited to facilitating rather than actively instructing in digital literacy. The myth allows them to downplay the need for sustained professional development, which is often time-consuming and underfunded. In systems where teachers are already overburdened, the narrative that students "already know how" to use technology becomes a tempting shortcut. Yet studies consistently show that without explicit instruction in evaluating online sources, managing digital projects, or applying technology creatively, students remain trapped at a superficial level of use. *The persistence of the myth in schools reflects not just misunderstanding but the structural realities of under-resourced educational systems searching for relief wherever they can find it.*

Policy plays its part by rewarding surface-level measures of progress. Governments eager to showcase modernisation often rely on visible, quantifiable indicators such as the number of laptops distributed or the percentage of schools with broadband access. These figures are easy to communicate, politically appealing, and lend themselves to bold declarations of digital inclusion. What they do not capture is whether students are actually developing competence, discernment, or creativity with these tools. Competence is difficult to measure and slow to cultivate, requiring sustained investment in teacher training, curriculum design, and long-term assessment. Exposure, by contrast, is straightforward to count. This dynamic incentivises policymakers to equate access with expertise, even when the evidence tells another story. The result is policy that celebrates devices in classrooms but neglects the ecosystems of support that make those devices meaningful.

Commercial interests have arguably been the strongest force in perpetuating the myth. For technology companies, the idea that young people are innately fluent is both flattering and profitable. It supports the belief that devices themselves unlock opportunity and that the latest hardware or platform is a ticket to future success. Marketing campaigns routinely showcase smiling children using tablets or laptops, reinforcing the impression that little more is required than exposure. The myth functions as a sales strategy, shifting attention away from the need for critical pedagogy or structural support. By selling the dream of effortless empowerment, companies avoid difficult conversations about inequality, distraction, or the risks of unmediated engagement. *The myth persists because it aligns so neatly with the commercial logic of selling products rather than cultivating literacy.*

The media has also played a role in sustaining the narrative. Popular articles often emphasise generational divides, portraying today's youth as inherently different because of their relationship with technology. Stories of toddlers navigating YouTube before they can read or teenagers coding apps in their bedrooms reinforce the idea of natural digital fluency. While such anecdotes are true in isolated cases, they create a distorted picture when applied to entire generations. The exceptional is mistaken for the norm, and the complexity of digital competence is flattened into spectacle. The media's fascination with technological precocity feeds cultural stereotypes and entrenches the divide between supposedly fluent youth and supposedly inept adults.

There is also an ideological dimension. The myth of the digital native dovetails with broader narratives of progress that equate technological advancement with human advancement. In societies that valorise innovation, it is attractive to believe that each new generation arrives pre-adapted to the tools of the future. The alternative—that education systems, families, and communities must work intentionally to cultivate competence—feels less glamorous and more burdensome. The myth simplifies the story of technological change, casting it as natural evolution rather than contested, uneven, and dependent on social structures. It transforms what should be a deliberate process of cultivation into a passive process of exposure, reinforcing the illusion that progress is automatic.

Yet perhaps the most striking reason the myth persists is that it contains a kernel of observable truth. Young people *do* appear more comfortable with devices than their elders. They adapt quickly to new platforms, absorb the mechanics of navigation intuitively, and often surpass adults in speed and ease. This comfort, however, is consistently misinterpreted as competence. The gap between the two is precisely what has been underestimated. The myth endures not because it is wholly false but because it is a half-truth—plausible enough to convince, seductive enough to spread, and simple enough to be believed. And half-truths, especially when they flatter cultural anxieties, are harder to dislodge than outright falsehoods.

The persistence of the myth carries real consequences. By treating comfort as competence, adults withhold guidance at the very moment it is most needed. By equating exposure with expertise, policymakers declare success prematurely, leaving structural inequalities unaddressed. By celebrating devices as educational revolutions, companies divert attention from the deeper work of fostering discernment, creativity, and critical thought. The result is a generation that appears prepared but remains under-equipped, and a society that congratulates itself on progress while leaving many of its students stranded on the surface of digital life.

Understanding why the myth persists is therefore more than an academic exercise. It is a reminder that myths endure not only because people misunderstand reality but because those myths serve functions: to reassure, to simplify, to sell, and to relieve. *The belief that exposure equals expertise survives because it is easier, more profitable, and less demanding than facing the harder truth—that expertise must be cultivated deliberately, and that without guidance, the digital age will widen divides rather than bridge them.* Only by recognising these forces can we begin to challenge the narratives that sustain the illusion and replace them with more honest, more demanding, and ultimately more empowering understandings of what digital competence really requires.

Chapter 2
Inequality in the Digital Age

The digital revolution promised a levelling of the playing field. Advocates spoke of technology as a universal solvent for inequality, a tool that could place the world's knowledge at every child's fingertips and free education from the constraints of geography or class. Yet as the dust of early optimism has settled, a more sobering picture has emerged. Technology, rather than dissolving inequality, has reconfigured it. The old divides of wealth, geography, and culture have not disappeared; they have been transposed into new digital registers. Broadband speed, device quality, subscription costs, and the subtler resources of guidance and household stability now dictate who reaps the benefits of digital learning and who remains locked out. *The story of the digital age is not simply one of access gained but of disparities multiplied, repackaged, and quietly entrenched.*

The most visible layer of this divide is infrastructure. In many developed nations, the assumption that every student is online has become commonplace, yet this masks enormous variation in the quality and reliability of access. Rural communities often endure patchy connections, throttled bandwidth, and prohibitively expensive service, creating conditions where students can log on but cannot stream lessons, collaborate in real time, or download the materials their peers take for granted. In low-income urban areas, families may share a single device among multiple children or rely on outdated machines that struggle to run contemporary software. The consequence is a paradox: formal access exists, but functional access does not. A student who takes half an hour to load a lesson because of poor bandwidth is technically "connected" but practically excluded. The infrastructure gap is thus not just a matter of on/off access but of quality, consistency, and affordability—dimensions that profoundly shape educational opportunity.

Less visible but equally corrosive are the hidden costs of access. Devices, once purchased, demand constant maintenance through upgrades, software subscriptions, and security updates. Many educational platforms rely on freemium models, offering basic functionality for free but reserving the most valuable features behind paywalls. Families who cannot afford recurring fees are left with a skeletal version of the tools that wealthier peers use to full effect. Similarly, the rapid cycle of device obsolescence creates pressure to replace hardware every few years, a burden that falls disproportionately on households already stretched thin. For middle-class families, these are routine but manageable expenses; for others, they are sources of quiet exclusion. The rhetoric of universal access obscures the reality that sustaining access is an ongoing economic strain, one that quietly widens the gap between those who can absorb hidden costs and those who cannot.

Schools, often heralded as the great equaliser, are themselves divided in how they deploy technology. In well-resourced schools, devices are integrated into project-based learning, collaborative research, and creative production, enriching education beyond the textbook. In underfunded schools, by contrast, the same devices are often deployed narrowly, serving as tools for drill-and-practice exercises or as platforms for standardised test preparation. The difference lies not in the hardware but in the vision, resources, and pedagogical culture surrounding it. When technology is used as enrichment, it amplifies curiosity and expands horizons; when it is used as a crutch for accountability metrics, it narrows education to the mechanics of test performance. *The same device can be a passport to creativity in one context and a cage of repetition in another, amplifying rather than diminishing educational divides.*

The home environment adds yet another layer of inequality, one that is often underestimated in policy discussions. A laptop in the bedroom of a child whose parents can guide them, set boundaries, and encourage exploration functions very differently from a laptop in a crowded household where multiple children compete for space and attention. Parental digital literacy plays a decisive role: some families can coach children in using technology responsibly and effectively, while others, lacking the same familiarity, either over-police use in ways that stifle exploration or abdicate responsibility altogether. Household rules, cultural attitudes towards technology, and even the availability of a quiet corner for study shape the educational value of digital tools as much as the specifications of the devices themselves. These factors cannot be solved through distribution schemes alone; they reveal that digital inequality is as much social and cultural as it is technological.

The persistence of these divides challenges the assumption that technology is a neutral force. Devices and networks are not dropped into a vacuum; they enter ecosystems already shaped by wealth, geography, culture, and institutional priorities. In some contexts, they serve as multipliers of opportunity, enabling students to pursue interests, build skills, and access resources far beyond their local environment. In others, they reinforce limitations, offering the illusion of modernity without its substance. A child in a well-resourced household may use a tablet to create a podcast, collaborate on international projects, or learn coding, while another, ostensibly equally equipped, may use the same device only for test drills or passive consumption of entertainment. Both are "connected," but only one is being positioned to thrive in the digital age.

The central argument of this chapter is that inequality in the digital age is not an incidental by-product of technology; it is an embedded feature of how technology interacts with existing social structures. Access is necessary but insufficient.

What matters are the conditions under which access is provided, the hidden costs attached to sustaining it, the institutional cultures that govern its use, and the household dynamics that frame its meaning. These factors combine to create a complex, layered system of digital inequality that cannot be addressed through devices and broadband alone. *To see technology as a universal equaliser is to mistake the surface for the substance; the reality is that it functions as both equaliser and amplifier, depending on the ecosystem into which it is introduced.*

This chapter will trace these dynamics with clarity and precision, unpacking how infrastructure, costs, schools, and homes shape the contours of opportunity in the digital age. By examining each layer, we can begin to understand not only why divides persist but why they are deepening, and why the myth of universal access conceals more than it reveals. The task ahead is not merely to connect students but to ensure that connections translate into competence, confidence, and creativity. To achieve that requires recognising that the digital divide is no longer a simple matter of who has devices and who does not; it is about the quality of infrastructure, the affordability of participation, the pedagogy of schools, and the supportiveness of homes. *Only by addressing these interlocking layers can we begin to turn technology from an amplifier of inequality into a genuine equaliser of opportunity.*

Infrastructure as the New Divide

The story of inequality in education is no longer written solely in the language of textbooks, class sizes, or teacher availability. It is increasingly measured in megabits per second, the number of devices per household, and the quality of the hardware that children use to connect to the wider world. A student's capacity to participate fully in learning is now tied to the speed of their broadband, the strength of their Wi-Fi signal, and the reliability of their device. The shift is subtle yet profound: where once the critical question was whether a child had access to a classroom at all, today it is whether the infrastructure of their digital environment enables or obstructs genuine learning. *Inequality has not disappeared; it has been redrawn through the circuitry of the digital age.*

The most obvious fault line is broadband access. Policymakers often announce coverage statistics—95 per cent of households connected, national rollouts of fibre optic networks, universal service commitments—but these figures conceal wide disparities in quality. In rural communities, "access" may mean a single unreliable connection that slows to a crawl during peak hours, rendering video-based learning impractical. Students in these areas frequently cannot participate in live classes, download large resources, or collaborate meaningfully with peers. The pandemic starkly revealed these limitations: when classrooms moved online, students in rural or low-income households were disproportionately absent, not because they lacked devices but because their connections simply could not support the demands of digital schooling. The difference between broadband in policy reports and broadband in practice is the difference between a world of opportunity and one of systemic exclusion.

Bandwidth, though often treated as a technical detail, is in fact a social determinant of educational opportunity. A child in a suburban home with high-speed fibre can simultaneously run video calls, access interactive simulations, and collaborate in real time without friction. A child in a rural household with a 3G connection may spend more time waiting for content to load than engaging with it. The educational gap this creates is not trivial; it accumulates daily, as some students build habits of exploration and collaboration while others internalise frustration and disengagement. *To speak of the digital divide as a binary—connected or unconnected—is to miss the reality that the quality of connection is as decisive as its existence.*

Device quality adds another layer to this infrastructure divide. A laptop that freezes during video editing or lacks the memory to run essential applications effectively undermines a student's capacity to engage. In low-income households, students may rely on older devices handed down from relatives or purchased at low cost, often with outdated operating systems and limited functionality. While their peers experiment with design software, data analysis tools, or advanced coding environments, these students are restricted to basic browsing and word processing. Smartphones, often the default device in poorer households, provide access of a kind but are ill-suited for complex academic tasks such as managing spreadsheets, writing extended essays, or engaging in collaborative projects that require multiple open windows. The consequence is a two-tiered experience: one in which technology opens doors to sophisticated forms of learning, and another in which it functions as a digital ceiling, limiting both aspiration and achievement.

Real-world examples illuminate the scale of the problem. In the United States, the Federal Communications Commission estimates that tens of millions of residents still lack reliable high-speed internet, disproportionately concentrated in rural communities and among low-income households. During the pandemic, stories abounded of children sitting in fast-food car parks to access Wi-Fi for their lessons, or sharing a single outdated laptop among siblings with conflicting schedules. In the United Kingdom, the government's emergency laptop distribution scheme revealed the inadequacy of the devices provided; many were too slow to handle video conferencing, forcing students into a cycle of dropped connections and incomplete participation. Meanwhile, in parts of sub-Saharan Africa, mobile data costs remain prohibitively high, meaning that even when families have smartphones, sustained use for education drains scarce household resources. These examples underscore a harsh truth: *infrastructure is not evenly distributed, and the absence of reliable, affordable, high-quality infrastructure locks students into systemic disadvantage.*

The problem is not only technical but cumulative. A student who repeatedly misses classes due to poor connectivity falls behind academically. A child who cannot complete assignments because their device lacks necessary software internalises a sense of inadequacy. Over time, these disadvantages crystallise into patterns of performance, shaping exam results, access to higher education, and eventually employment opportunities. In this sense, the infrastructure divide functions not merely as an inconvenience but as a mechanism of social stratification. It ensures that those born into households and communities with weaker infrastructure are systematically less able to convert exposure to technology into genuine competence and opportunity. The digital age promised to flatten hierarchies; instead, it has woven them more deeply into the fabric of everyday life.

Contrasting perspectives often emerge in discussions of this issue. Some argue that infrastructure is improving rapidly, with initiatives to expand fibre networks and mobile coverage promising to narrow gaps over time. Others point out that technological advancement often accelerates inequalities: as the bandwidth needs of modern applications increase, those already struggling to keep up fall further behind. A decade ago, a basic connection might have sufficed for text-based resources; today, interactive platforms, high-resolution video, and collaborative tools demand speeds that stretch the capacity of underdeveloped networks. The definition of "adequate" infrastructure shifts constantly upward, ensuring that those at the margins are in a perpetual state of catch-up. *Progress for some can mean entrenchment for others, unless policy addresses the pace of technological change as well as its distribution.*

Policy responses have frequently focused on closing gaps in coverage rather than in quality. Subsidised broadband programmes, while laudable, often fail to address the hidden costs of data overages, the expense of upgrading routers, or the practical limitations of outdated networks. Device distribution schemes may provide machines but not the technical support or replacement cycles required to sustain their use. Without long-term planning, such initiatives risk becoming symbolic gestures rather than transformative solutions. The deeper challenge lies in recognising that infrastructure is not simply a matter of laying cables or handing out devices but of creating ecosystems that allow students to thrive. This includes maintenance, training, and ongoing investment—not just initial access.

The persistence of the infrastructure divide invites reflection on how societies conceptualise equity. For centuries, education systems have grappled with how to provide equal opportunity despite unequal circumstances. The digital age has added a new dimension: even when schools are well-staffed and curricula well-designed, a weak internet connection or an inadequate device can undermine all other efforts. Infrastructure has become the new baseline of equity, the silent determinant that enables or constrains all other forms of educational endeavour. To ignore it is to accept that opportunity will remain stratified by geography and income, despite the rhetoric of universal access.

The philosophical insight here is that technology, often portrayed as neutral, is in fact deeply relational. A device's meaning lies not in its existence but in the context that surrounds it: the speed of the network, the affordability of upgrades, the support structures available. Infrastructure does not simply connect; it mediates, shapes, and ultimately decides whether access is empowering or hollow. *Inequality in the digital age is built not only on who owns devices but on how those devices function in practice, in the granular details of bandwidth, latency, and durability.*

The infrastructure divide is not glamorous. It does not lend itself to triumphant headlines or celebratory photo opportunities. But it is decisive. Until societies confront the uneven distribution of broadband, bandwidth, and device quality, the promise of digital learning will remain an illusion for millions. Infrastructure is the foundation on which all other aspects of digital equity rest. If it is weak or uneven, the edifice of opportunity collapses. If it is strong and sustained, students can begin to move from mere access towards meaningful competence and opportunity.

Hidden Costs of Access

The conversation around digital access often ends at the point of connection. Policymakers celebrate rising broadband coverage, charities campaign for device distribution, and schools announce successful laptop rollouts. On paper, these initiatives appear transformative. Yet beneath the surface lies an economic reality that is less visible but equally decisive: the ongoing, compounding costs of staying connected. Subscription models, application fees, data charges, and the relentless cycle of device obsolescence create financial demands that disproportionately burden families with fewer resources. *Access is not a single hurdle overcome once; it is a recurring expense that quietly widens the very gaps technology was meant to close.*

The shift from ownership to subscription in digital services is central to this hidden economy. Where once a one-time software purchase granted indefinite use, today's students must navigate a landscape dominated by monthly or annual fees. Productivity suites, cloud storage, collaborative platforms, and even basic educational tools now operate on subscription models. A family may provide a child with a laptop, but without the necessary licences for word processing, spreadsheet analysis, or presentation software, the device becomes severely limited. Educational institutions often negotiate bulk licences, but outside school hours, students are expected to sustain access individually, especially as assignments increasingly rely on cloud-based collaboration. For wealthier families, these costs are background noise; for those with tight budgets, they accumulate into barriers. The consequence is a subtle but significant form of exclusion: students may have the hardware yet still lack the means to participate fully in the digital classroom.

The rise of app-based learning compounds the issue. Educational platforms, gamified learning tools, and study aids often entice with free entry points but reserve meaningful content or advanced features behind paywalls. What begins as an apparently accessible solution quickly becomes a financial strain when multiplied across subjects and children. Language learning apps, coding tutorials, and maths support platforms, while marketed as universally available, frequently operate under freemium models that reward those who can pay and frustrate those who cannot. This dynamic creates a two-tiered system: one group of students benefits from rich, personalised digital resources, while another is left with watered-down versions or constant prompts to upgrade. *The very platforms designed to democratise learning often re-inscribe inequality through their economic design.*

Device obsolescence represents another dimension of hidden cost. Manufacturers design products with limited lifespans, whether through non-replaceable batteries, software updates that strain older hardware, or ecosystems that encourage continual upgrading. In wealthier households, a three-year replacement cycle is common, ensuring children have up-to-date machines capable of running demanding applications. In lower-income households, devices are kept long after their practical lifespan, forcing students to struggle with slow load times, incompatibility issues, or outright system failures. The experience of trying to complete assignments on outdated equipment is more than inconvenient; it undermines confidence, efficiency, and performance. The concept of "digital access" loses meaning if the tools provided are inadequate for the tasks expected.

Data costs add yet another layer, particularly in regions where mobile networks are the primary means of connection. In parts of sub-Saharan Africa, South Asia, and Latin America, households spend significant portions of their income on mobile data. Educational platforms that assume continuous connectivity inadvertently impose recurring costs that are unsustainable for many families. Even in wealthier countries, households without reliable broadband often resort to mobile hotspots, racking up bills that silently strain budgets. For students, this creates difficult trade-offs: choosing which assignments to prioritise, limiting participation in live classes, or rationing screen time to manage data consumption. *The cost of access is not only financial but cognitive, as students are forced to make choices their wealthier peers never face.*

Case studies illustrate the breadth of this problem. During the COVID-19 pandemic, when schools shifted online, British surveys revealed that many low-income families could not afford the data required for daily video lessons, even when devices were provided. Telecom providers eventually offered discounted or zero-rated access to educational platforms, but only after months of disruption. In the United States, some school districts attempted to issue Wi-Fi hotspots to families, yet monthly data caps often left students disconnected before the end of the month. In India, where smartphone access is widespread, the cost of sustained online learning led many families to withdraw children from digital lessons altogether, prioritising scarce household resources for food and essentials. These examples reveal that *the barrier is not the absence of access but the cost of maintaining it consistently.*

The hidden costs of access are not evenly distributed. Middle- and upper-class families often absorb them without much thought, normalising subscriptions, upgrades, and data plans as part of household budgets. Lower-income families, by contrast, must constantly weigh these expenses against other necessities, creating a precarious balance that leaves students vulnerable to disruption. This divide is subtle but powerful. It rarely appears in official statistics, because the families are technically "connected," yet in practice they experience digital learning as fragile, unstable, and conditional. *The narrative of universal access masks the reality of unequal sustainability.*

Philosophically, these dynamics force a reconsideration of what equity means in the digital age. Providing a device or an internet connection does not in itself guarantee equal opportunity if ongoing costs make access fragile. True equity must account for the sustainability of participation, not just its initiation. It must ask whether students can rely on their digital tools consistently, or whether their educational experience is constantly interrupted by expired licences, outdated hardware, or depleted data. *Access is not a binary condition; it is a spectrum shaped by recurring demands that are easier for some to shoulder than others.*

The issue also raises questions of responsibility. Should schools and governments absorb the costs of essential subscriptions and updates, ensuring all students can participate fully, or should these be left to families? Should technology companies rethink models that monetise learning through exclusionary paywalls, or is this simply the logic of the market? Different contexts provide different answers. In some Nordic countries, schools provide not only devices but licences and technical support, embedding digital access within the public education system. In others, particularly in lower-income nations, the burden falls almost entirely on families, perpetuating cycles of inequality. The contrast illustrates that these hidden costs are not inevitable; they are the result of choices about how technology is designed, funded, and distributed.

What makes the hidden costs so pernicious is their invisibility. Policymakers can celebrate laptop distributions or broadband expansion while overlooking the quieter, ongoing expenses that limit real participation. Schools can claim universal access while ignoring the fact that some students cannot afford the software required to complete assignments. Companies can present themselves as democratisers of knowledge while profiting from subscription models that exclude those who cannot pay. *The narrative of progress is maintained because the exclusions are diffuse, individualised, and less visible than the triumph of initial access.*

For students, however, the effects are immediate and tangible. Falling behind because an app subscription expired, missing deadlines because a device crashed, rationing screen time to save data—all these experiences accumulate into disadvantage. Over time, they shape confidence, performance, and aspiration, entrenching educational divides that are harder to detect but no less damaging than those of the pre-digital era. Access, in its hidden costs, becomes a new frontier of inequality—one that requires as much attention as infrastructure and pedagogy if digital learning is to fulfil its promise.

School as a Tech Equalizer—or Amplifier

The promise of educational technology has always been framed in universalist terms. Advocates present digital tools as levellers, capable of providing every child with access to the same resources regardless of geography or income. Yet schools, far from being neutral channels for these tools, shape their use in ways that can either mitigate or exacerbate inequality. The very same devices, platforms, and programmes can be engines of enrichment in one institution and instruments of reduction in another. *The decisive factor is not the technology itself but how schools deploy it: as an invitation to explore, create, and think critically, or as a mechanism for control, drill, and compliance.*

The contrast is often stark. In well-resourced schools, technology is woven into rich pedagogical frameworks. Students might use laptops to collaborate on documentaries, analyse live datasets, or engage in cross-border projects with peers around the world. Here, devices extend learning beyond the classroom, enabling children to experience themselves as producers of knowledge rather than mere recipients. In these contexts, digital tools function as amplifiers of curiosity and imagination, providing scaffolding for higher-order skills that resonate far beyond school walls. The atmosphere is one of experimentation and discovery, with technology framed as a partner in intellectual growth.

By contrast, in underfunded schools—often serving disadvantaged communities—technology is too frequently repurposed as a vehicle for standardisation. Devices are programmed with test-preparation apps, used to deliver worksheets electronically, or deployed to monitor attendance and compliance. Students may spend hours clicking through multiple-choice quizzes or filling in digital blanks, with little opportunity to create, analyse, or question. In these settings, technology functions less as a catalyst for enrichment than as a convenient means of control. What is celebrated as "innovation" in one environment is experienced as monotony in another. *The paradox is that the same machine that empowers some to explore complex ideas is used to drill others into minimum standards.*

Evidence underscores this divide. Studies from the OECD and UNESCO have highlighted that while students with access to creative digital use show gains in problem-solving and collaborative skills, those exposed primarily to test-prep software often demonstrate little improvement, and sometimes even declines, in higher-order thinking. For example, a study in the United States found that high-income schools were more likely to integrate project-based uses of technology, while low-income schools disproportionately adopted software designed for remediation and exam preparation. The structural result is clear: technology widens rather than narrows the gap between students depending on whether it is treated as enrichment or as enforcement.

The dynamics behind these differences are complex. Teacher training plays a critical role. Educators in well-supported schools often receive sustained professional development that enables them to integrate technology thoughtfully into their curricula. They are encouraged to take risks, share practices, and adapt tools to fit pedagogical goals. In contrast, teachers in underfunded schools may be handed devices without sufficient guidance, pressured to use them primarily for measurable outcomes such as test scores. With accountability frameworks tied to standardised results, technology becomes a means of meeting external demands rather than of deepening learning. *The institutional culture surrounding technology is as important as the devices themselves.*

Funding structures further shape these outcomes. Wealthier schools can invest in high-quality platforms, ensure devices are regularly upgraded, and employ dedicated IT staff who support teachers in experimenting with new approaches. Poorer schools often lack the resources for such infrastructure, leading to outdated devices, unreliable networks, and limited technical support. Even when hardware is available, the quality of implementation is undermined by logistical challenges. A tablet that freezes or a Wi-Fi connection that fails mid-lesson quickly erodes teacher confidence and narrows possibilities, encouraging reliance on low-demand applications that require less stability but also provide less educational value.

Cultural expectations also influence how technology is positioned. Parents in affluent communities may lobby schools to introduce coding, robotics, or digital storytelling as pathways to future opportunity. Their advocacy reinforces a vision of technology as a tool for empowerment. In disadvantaged communities, where parents may themselves have limited digital literacy, the demand is often framed differently—towards basic proficiency or test performance. Schools respond to these perceived expectations, tailoring their technology strategies accordingly. *The result is a feedback loop in which community assumptions and school practices reinforce each other, embedding different trajectories of technological use.*

Case studies highlight these divergent realities. In Finland, where education policy prioritises equity and teacher autonomy, technology is integrated into holistic projects that connect subjects and cultivate critical inquiry. A history class might involve building interactive timelines, drawing on multiple sources and digital archives, encouraging both content mastery and digital discernment. Meanwhile, in parts of the United States, large urban districts have contracted with companies to provide computerised "personalised learning" platforms that break content into small, testable units. Teachers are instructed to monitor dashboards rather than to design creative tasks, shifting their role towards supervision rather than facilitation. Both settings claim to be "digitally advanced," yet the experiences and outcomes for students are radically different.

The philosophical question underlying these contrasts is whether schools view technology as a means of broadening horizons or as a tool of efficiency. The former requires investment, imagination, and trust in teachers; the latter seeks predictability, measurement, and cost-effectiveness. Neither approach is neutral, for each reflects underlying assumptions about what education is for. In treating students as innovators-in-training, schools prepare them for agency in a digital society. In treating them as data points to be raised towards minimum standards, they prepare them for compliance. *Technology does not dictate these choices; schools do.*

It is tempting to believe that simply expanding access to devices and platforms will equalise opportunities, but the evidence shows otherwise. Without deliberate attention to pedagogy, culture, and support, technology tends to mirror existing inequalities in the school system. Those with resources, autonomy, and vision use it to enrich; those constrained by accountability pressures and limited funding use it to reinforce minimum thresholds. In effect, technology becomes a magnifying glass, enlarging whatever practices already dominate within a school.

The challenge, then, is not only to provide technology but to ensure that schools deploy it as an equaliser rather than an amplifier of inequality. This requires rethinking professional development, aligning accountability measures with broader learning goals, and resisting the temptation to treat digital tools as substitutes for human teaching. It also demands recognition that *what matters is not whether schools have technology but how they choose to use it.* The dividing line between enrichment and reduction, between opportunity and constraint, runs not through the devices themselves but through the cultures, priorities, and practices of schools.

If schools are to serve as genuine equalisers, technology must be embedded in contexts that value creativity, critical thought, and exploration. Otherwise, the same devices that symbolise modernity risk becoming the silent agents of stratification, deepening divides under the guise of progress.

The Home Environment Gap

The popular narrative around digital inequality often focuses on infrastructure—broadband speeds, device distribution, and the reach of connectivity. Yet another layer of inequality, often less visible but no less decisive, lies within the home. The household is the first and most enduring learning environment, and in the digital age, its role has become amplified. Whether students thrive or falter in making use of digital tools depends not only on the machines they hold in their hands but on the guidance they receive, the spaces available to them, and the rules or norms that govern their use. *The home environment shapes outcomes as powerfully as any classroom intervention, and disparities here are as consequential as disparities in school funding or technological infrastructure.*

Parental guidance is the most significant of these factors. Digital competence does not emerge automatically from exposure to devices; it is cultivated through instruction, modelling, and feedback. Parents with higher levels of digital literacy are more likely to coach their children in discerning credible information, managing online risks, and using technology creatively rather than passively. They can explain the difference between researching a topic and simply scrolling through search results, or between curating content and consuming whatever is algorithmically delivered. This kind of scaffolding transforms comfort into competence. By contrast, parents who lack confidence with technology may adopt one of two approaches: laissez-faire indulgence, leaving children to their own devices, or restrictive prohibition, policing screen time without offering guidance in responsible use. Both approaches fail to provide the mentoring necessary for students to develop agency in digital spaces. *The home is not merely where devices are located; it is where digital habits are formed, reinforced, or neglected.*

Space within the household further compounds these differences. A child with a quiet room and personal device is positioned very differently from one sharing a small living space with siblings, competing for time on a shared laptop or tablet. In cramped or noisy environments, focus becomes a scarce resource, and learning is fragmented by interruptions. The pandemic made these realities visible on a global scale. While some children attended remote classes from dedicated study corners, others joined lessons from cars parked outside Wi-Fi hotspots, or from kitchens doubling as classrooms. Educational technologists may design platforms for "anytime, anywhere" learning, but in practice, the quality of the physical environment remains a decisive factor. *A laptop in a bedroom with parental support is not the same educational resource as a laptop in a crowded living room with no one to guide its use.*

Household rules and cultural attitudes also shape digital outcomes. Some families establish structured routines around screen use, integrating technology into balanced daily schedules. Devices are treated as tools, not distractions, and norms around appropriate use are consistently reinforced. Other households, whether through lack of awareness or lack of time, allow unregulated use, where learning competes with endless streams of entertainment. In such cases, the very presence of devices can undermine educational focus rather than enhance it. The difference between digital empowerment and digital distraction often lies not in the technology itself but in the frameworks of expectation and accountability established at home. Where guidance is strong, students learn to regulate attention and engage critically; where it is weak, devices become instruments of avoidance or overindulgence.

Socioeconomic status amplifies these dynamics. Families with resources can purchase ergonomic furniture, provide multiple devices, and invest in high-quality educational apps or tutoring. They may even hire digital coaches or enrol children in coding academies, embedding digital competence as a form of cultural capital. By contrast, lower-income households may struggle to keep up with hidden costs, lack private study spaces, and be unable to supervise use due to demanding work schedules. The consequence is that children from wealthier homes receive not just better infrastructure but richer contexts for making use of it. *The home environment gap is not about whether children own devices but about the conditions under which those devices are embedded in everyday life.*

The intergenerational divide adds complexity. Parents who grew up in analogue contexts often view technology through the lens of risk, focusing on dangers such as online predators, cyberbullying, or addiction. Their rules may centre on restriction—limiting time, blocking websites—without parallel emphasis on opportunity. Younger parents, by contrast, may be more inclined to see devices as educational tools but may lack the knowledge to filter quality from distraction. In both cases, children are often left without systematic guidance in developing digital discernment. Research from the EU Kids Online project has shown that while parents across Europe routinely restrict internet use, far fewer actively engage in co-learning or mentorship. The imbalance between policing and coaching leaves many children competent in entertainment but unskilled in critical evaluation.

Case studies highlight the weight of these home dynamics. In Singapore, a government initiative to integrate digital literacy into family life encouraged parents to participate in workshops alongside their children, with notable improvements in how households managed technology. By contrast, in parts of the United States, low-income students reported spending hours completing assignments on smartphones because their parents, working multiple jobs, could not provide laptops or supervise usage. The gap in outcomes was not explained by access alone but by the interplay of space, support, and guidance. These examples reveal that *the home environment is both the most intimate and the most overlooked dimension of digital inequality.*

The philosophical dimension of this issue lies in redefining responsibility. For decades, schools have been seen as the primary engines of education, while homes provided background support. In the digital age, however, the boundary between school and home has blurred. Homework is digital, collaboration happens online, and platforms extend learning into evenings and weekends. This means that *home environments now directly co-produce educational outcomes,* not merely support them. The distribution of guidance, space, and rules across households is therefore as central to equity as the distribution of teachers or textbooks. Ignoring this reality risks treating education as something that happens only in schools, when in fact it is increasingly co-shaped by domestic conditions.

Addressing the home environment gap requires more than distributing devices; it requires strategies to support families in their role as co-educators. This could include parental training in digital literacy, school–home partnerships that provide structured guidance, and community initiatives that create shared learning spaces for children lacking quiet corners at home. Crucially, it also requires a cultural shift away from the idea that children are self-sufficient in digital contexts. Comfort is not competence, and unsupervised exposure is not empowerment. Without intentional guidance, digital environments are more likely to reproduce passivity and distraction than to cultivate agency and opportunity.

The home environment gap underscores the limits of access-focused thinking. A child with broadband and a laptop may still be at a disadvantage if their home lacks the guidance, routines, and space necessary to use those tools effectively. Conversely, a child with modest infrastructure but strong parental mentorship may flourish, developing digital confidence and resilience that far outstrip their peers. The household, in all its variation, has become one of the most important determinants of educational equity in the digital age. To ignore it is to accept that inequality will continue to be reproduced not only between schools but within homes themselves.

Chapter 3
Literacy in the Age of Algorithms

Literacy has always been a marker of power. The ability to read and write once separated the ruling classes from the ruled, opening access to religious texts, political discourse, and economic opportunity. For centuries, campaigns for universal literacy were driven not only by the ideal of individual enlightenment but by the recognition that those who could not read or write were effectively excluded from civic life. Today, however, the definition of literacy is shifting again. To be "literate" in the twenty-first century is no longer solely about decoding print on a page. It is about navigating a digital environment that is vast, fragmented, and algorithmically curated. *The critical question is not just whether students can consume digital information, but whether they can evaluate its credibility, understand how it is shaped, and create knowledge within it rather than simply replicate what they encounter.*

The internet promised boundless knowledge, yet its vastness is filtered through invisible systems. Search engines do not simply retrieve information; they rank it, prioritising some sources while burying others. Social media feeds do not reflect reality in its fullness but tailor streams of content designed to maximise engagement. Recommendation systems, driven by algorithms optimised for profit rather than pedagogy, decide what appears before our eyes. For students, this means that what they "know" is already a product of design. Their exploration of the world is subtly channelled, often narrowing horizons rather than broadening them. The skill once required to locate information in libraries—patience, cross-referencing, discernment—has been replaced by the illusion of ease. *To type a query and receive an instant answer feels empowering, but without critical literacy, students become dependent on systems that hide as much as they reveal.*

The challenge of digital literacy, then, is not only about information access but about discernment. Consider the prevalence of "copy-paste culture" in classrooms. The abundance of online material makes it effortless to replicate work rather than engage deeply with it. Plagiarism is not simply a moral failure but a symptom of a wider educational shift: when tools reward speed and convenience, reflection and originality are sidelined. A student who can compile a project by collating Wikipedia entries or AI-generated summaries may appear digitally competent, but their skill set is brittle. They have learned to gather but not to sift, to reproduce but not to question. The temptation of shortcuts erodes the habits of patience and perseverance that underpin meaningful learning. *Critical thinking, in this environment, is not a luxury but a survival skill.*

At the heart of this transformation is a hierarchy of digital literacy that is rarely acknowledged but profoundly consequential. At the base are students who engage with technology primarily as consumers—scrolling, streaming, downloading. They are comfortable but not competent. Higher up the hierarchy are those who are guided, often by parents or educators, to interrogate sources, compare perspectives, and evaluate credibility. They learn that the top result on a search engine is not necessarily the most reliable, that "viral" does not mean true, and that algorithms have agendas. At the very top are students who not only navigate and evaluate but also create: they code, design, publish, and contribute. These students move beyond passive consumption into active authorship, cultivating a sense of agency in the digital world. *The distribution of students across this hierarchy is not random; it reflects disparities of guidance, culture, and opportunity that mirror broader social inequalities.*

Examples abound of how this hierarchy manifests in practice. In classrooms where teachers explicitly teach digital discernment—examining how search results are ranked, dissecting the motives behind clickbait, or analysing the difference between peer-reviewed research and opinion blogs—students develop long-term advantages. They are not only better at academic tasks but more confident in navigating the digital workplace, where evaluating the credibility of information is an everyday requirement. By contrast, students left to "figure it out" often mistake fluency with social media for fluency with knowledge. They may appear confident in navigating platforms but struggle to distinguish fact from misinformation, or to resist the persuasive design of addictive feeds. *The myth of the "digital native" obscures the fact that digital literacy is unevenly distributed, and that without guidance, comfort can conceal shallow competence.*

The stakes are high because algorithms increasingly mediate not just information but identity. Young people growing up in algorithmically curated environments encounter echo chambers that reinforce biases, recommendation systems that feed them more of what they already like, and filter bubbles that limit their exposure to diverse perspectives. The educational consequence is profound: students risk mistaking familiarity for truth, equating repetition with reliability. A literacy curriculum that fails to address this reality is incomplete. Just as earlier generations were taught to read critically—interrogating authorship, bias, and intent—today's students must be taught to read the digital world critically, understanding not only content but the structures that shape it. *To be digitally literate in the age of algorithms is to see beyond the surface, to recognise that what appears neutral is in fact curated, selective, and shaped by hidden incentives.*

Yet there is also opportunity in this shift. The very tools that constrain can also liberate when approached with discernment. Students who learn to reverse-engineer algorithms, to trace the logic of a feed, or to map networks of influence gain a level of agency that transforms their relationship with technology. Rather than passive recipients of digital flows, they become conscious navigators. Rather than succumbing to copy-paste shortcuts, they cultivate originality and synthesis. This kind of literacy is not about rejecting technology but about inhabiting it with awareness. *It is the difference between being swept along by digital currents and learning how to swim within them.*

The broader lesson is that literacy in the digital age cannot be reduced to a checklist of technical skills. It is a form of cultural and intellectual empowerment, shaping how students think, interact, and create. Just as reading once enabled access to citizenship, digital literacy now enables access to opportunity in a society governed by data, algorithms, and information flows. The challenge for educators, policymakers, and families is to ensure that digital literacy is not stratified along lines of privilege, leaving some students fluent in discernment while others remain trapped in passive consumption. This chapter begins from the recognition that *literacy today is layered, contested, and consequential*, and that those who climb higher on the hierarchy of discernment and creation will enjoy long-term advantages in both academic and professional life.

The question is no longer whether students are online but whether they are truly literate within the systems that now shape knowledge. To answer it requires moving beyond simplistic assumptions of digital fluency and towards a richer understanding of what it means to think, question, and create in the age of algorithms. This is not merely an academic challenge; it is a civic one. Literacy has always been the foundation of participation. In the digital century, that foundation must be rebuilt, not in the ink of textbooks but in the critical discernment of digital citizens.

Beyond Reading and Writing

To describe a young person today as "literate" in the traditional sense is increasingly inadequate. The ability to decode printed text and produce coherent writing remains foundational, but it is no longer sufficient to navigate a world in which knowledge, communication, and participation are mediated by digital platforms. A child who can read novels fluently and compose essays by hand may still falter when confronted with the sprawling, contradictory, and algorithmically shaped universe of online information. *Literacy in the digital age is not about accessing content but about making sense of it, questioning it, and contributing to it. The line between reader and writer, consumer and creator, has blurred, and education must evolve to reflect that reality.*

The internet has democratised publishing to an unprecedented degree. Where once a handful of gatekeepers controlled the flow of information through books, newspapers, and broadcast channels, today anyone with a device can disseminate their views to a global audience. This has created both an extraordinary expansion of voices and a flood of noise. For the learner, the challenge is no longer scarcity but abundance. Digital literacy, therefore, requires the capacity to filter—to distinguish between peer-reviewed research and conspiracy theories, between authentic voices and manufactured propaganda, between credible expertise and persuasive but unfounded opinion. *Being able to read words on a screen is meaningless if one cannot interrogate their reliability or intent.*

Consider the case of search engines. A simple query produces millions of results, ranked by opaque algorithms that reflect commercial interests, popularity signals, and design choices rather than truth. Students often assume the first few results are the best, rarely scrolling further or questioning why certain pages appear at the top. The skill of locating knowledge has shifted: it is no longer about knowing where to look but about knowing how to assess what one finds. Teachers report that many students cite dubious blogs or unverified forums as sources with the same confidence they would attribute to academic journals. Without explicit instruction, digital natives are often digital naïves when it comes to discernment. *To be digitally literate is to understand that the architecture of the internet shapes not only what one sees but how one thinks.*

Yet digital literacy is not confined to evaluation; it extends to creation. The most empowered learners are those who not only consume content but produce it. Blogging, podcasting, coding, video editing, and collaborative knowledge-building platforms allow students to move from passive recipients to active contributors. In doing so, they acquire not just technical skills but a deeper understanding of audience, credibility, and ethics. A student who constructs a Wikipedia entry, for instance, must grapple with sourcing, neutrality, and the responsibilities of authorship. A teenager who publishes a video online learns about the dynamics of visibility, feedback, and digital permanence. These acts of creation demand reflection in a way that consumption does not. *True digital literacy requires not just fluency in reading digital environments but agency in shaping them.*

The hierarchy of digital engagement is revealing. At its base are students who scroll, swipe, and stream, participating primarily as consumers of entertainment. Higher up are those who interrogate, compare, and evaluate, cultivating discernment. At the top are those who create, combining technical fluency with critical awareness. Movement up this hierarchy is not automatic; it depends on guided practice, cultural capital, and institutional support. Wealthier students are more likely to be nudged towards creation—through coding camps, digital storytelling workshops, or mentorship in media production—while disadvantaged students may remain confined to passive consumption. The divide is therefore not just about access to devices but about access to meaningful uses of them. *Digital literacy is stratified, and the consequences of that stratification echo into higher education, employment, and civic life.*

Real-world examples illustrate these dynamics vividly. In Estonia, where digital skills are embedded into national curricula, students learn not only how to use platforms but how to question and build them, contributing to the country's reputation as a leader in digital governance. In contrast, research in the United States has shown that low-income students are often channelled into remedial programmes using drill-based software, reinforcing minimal proficiency rather than encouraging critical or creative engagement. Both groups may spend similar hours on devices, but their outcomes diverge sharply: one group develops agency, the other dependence. *The question is not how much time students spend with technology, but what they are guided to do with it.*

Plagiarism provides a further lens into the complexities of digital literacy. The ease of copying and pasting online content has transformed academic dishonesty into an everyday temptation. But plagiarism in the digital age is more than theft; it reflects a deeper issue of literacy. Many students do not fully grasp the boundaries between appropriation, remixing, and original authorship in environments where sharing and replication are normalised. Platforms encourage re-posting, meme culture thrives on adaptation, and citation practices vary widely across contexts. To cultivate digital literacy is not only to warn against plagiarism but to teach the ethics of digital authorship—how to credit, how to transform, how to innovate responsibly in an interconnected ecosystem. *The moral language of cheating is insufficient; what is needed is an expanded pedagogy of authorship for the digital age.*

The urgency of digital literacy also stems from its civic implications. Democracies depend on informed citizens capable of distinguishing fact from misinformation. Yet misinformation now spreads with unprecedented speed, often cloaked in the aesthetics of credibility. Deepfakes, manipulated statistics, and coordinated disinformation campaigns make it increasingly difficult to separate truth from falsehood. Students who cannot evaluate sources are not merely at a disadvantage academically; they are vulnerable as citizens. By contrast, those who learn to navigate digital information critically become resilient participants in public life. *Digital literacy is therefore not simply a private skill but a public necessity, as vital to the health of democracies as traditional literacy was to the rise of nation-states.*

Philosophically, this evolution challenges us to reconsider what it means to be educated. For centuries, literacy was synonymous with autonomy—the ability to read the world and write oneself into it. In the digital century, that autonomy is threatened not by illiteracy in the old sense but by partial literacy in the new one. A person may be fluent in reading and writing text yet be unable to resist algorithmic manipulation, to question the credibility of sources, or to contribute responsibly to digital discourse. *The literate subject of the twenty-first century must be equipped not only to interpret the written word but to navigate systems of information shaped by algorithms, corporations, and collective networks.*

The implications for education are profound. Schools that continue to treat literacy as reading and writing alone risk preparing students for a world that no longer exists. Curricula must expand to include digital evaluation, critical thinking about algorithms, and opportunities for creation. This does not mean abandoning traditional literacy; indeed, strong reading and writing remain the foundation for critical digital skills. But it does mean rethinking literacy as a continuum rather than a binary, one that ranges from decoding text to decoding systems, from composing essays to composing digital media, from reading passively to reading critically and writing actively in a networked world.

To be literate today is to possess the ability to locate knowledge in a flood of information, to evaluate it in light of credibility and context, and to contribute meaningfully to the ongoing production of ideas. This is not an optional enrichment but a core competency. Without it, students risk being not only consumers rather than creators, but subjects rather than citizens in a world governed by digital systems. With it, they gain the tools to engage, to question, and to shape the environments that shape them. *Beyond reading and writing lies the literacy that defines the twenty-first century: the capacity to think critically, act responsibly, and create with agency in the age of algorithms.*

The Algorithmic Trap

Knowledge has never been as abundant, accessible, and instant as it is today. With a swipe or a keystroke, students can access more information than the greatest scholars of the past could have gathered in a lifetime. Yet this abundance hides a paradox: while the digital world appears infinite, the paths that students actually walk are often startlingly narrow. Recommendation systems and search engines—those invisible curators of the online experience—do not simply deliver information; they structure it, filter it, and rank it in ways that shape what people come to know and believe. *The danger is that students mistake algorithmic curation for unmediated reality, failing to recognise that what they see online is not the world but a version of it tailored for them.*

Consider the simplicity of a Google search. A child typing a question receives an answer in less than a second. To the untrained eye, the results appear to be a neutral catalogue of knowledge. But every ranked list is a hierarchy of choices. Commercial imperatives, search engine optimisation tactics, and behavioural data all influence which results rise to the top. Students rarely scroll beyond the first page, and studies show that even university undergraduates often treat the first three links as inherently trustworthy. This creates a subtle distortion: not only do they accept the most visible information as the most reliable, but they also rarely encounter alternative perspectives buried deeper in the results. *The convenience of algorithms comes at the cost of diversity, depth, and doubt.*

Recommendation systems intensify this narrowing effect. Social media platforms, video-sharing sites, and even educational apps are designed to maximise engagement. Their goal is not to expand a learner's horizon but to hold attention. As a result, algorithms feed users more of what they already like, nudging them towards predictable patterns of consumption. A teenager researching climate change may be led to sensationalist content because it generates more clicks than measured scientific explanations. Another exploring history might encounter politicised narratives that confirm biases rather than challenge them. Over time, these algorithmically tailored feeds create what scholars call "filter bubbles"—personalised echo chambers that reinforce familiarity and suppress dissonance. *What students perceive as exploration is often a loop, circling them back to the same themes, voices, and assumptions.*

The trap is particularly dangerous because it feels empowering. To navigate an endless feed or to receive personalised suggestions creates the illusion of choice, when in fact the range of options has already been constrained. This is not to suggest malice on the part of all technology companies—many genuinely seek to provide useful, relevant recommendations—but the structural incentives of attention-driven design bias the system towards reinforcement rather than expansion. The logic is simple: people are more likely to click on content that resonates with their existing interests or fears. Over time, algorithms "learn" these preferences and deliver more of the same. The result is a cycle of narrowing horizons dressed in the guise of infinite possibility. *Students think they are accessing the world, but the world they see has been algorithmically pruned to fit them.*

Case studies illustrate the consequences. In 2018, a Pew Research Center study revealed that a significant number of American teenagers reported learning about news primarily through YouTube recommendations. Researchers found that the platform often led users from mainstream news content to more polarised or conspiratorial videos within just a few clicks. Similarly, an investigation into TikTok's algorithm showed that within minutes of interacting with certain hashtags, young users were inundated with related content, often extreme in tone or perspective. These patterns are not unique to entertainment platforms; they extend into educational contexts. Adaptive learning systems, designed to personalise instruction, sometimes reduce students' exposure to challenging material, keeping them within comfort zones that maximise completion metrics rather than fostering intellectual stretch. *Algorithms designed for engagement can inadvertently diminish the very curiosity and resilience that education is meant to cultivate.*

There is also a socio-economic dimension to the algorithmic trap. Students from affluent households often have adults who can guide them, contextualise digital information, and introduce them to diverse sources. They may be enrolled in schools where digital literacy is explicitly taught, helping them to see algorithms not as neutral arbiters but as systems to be understood and questioned. By contrast, students in less advantaged contexts are more likely to take algorithmic feeds at face value, mistaking them for objective mirrors of reality. This asymmetry creates long-term consequences. Those who learn to navigate and critique algorithms develop agency; those who do not remain passive consumers. *The algorithmic trap is not evenly distributed—it compounds existing educational and cultural inequalities.*

Philosophically, this raises an unsettling question about the nature of knowledge in the digital age. For centuries, education was built on the premise that learners could access the same body of texts, enabling shared reference points for civic and intellectual life. The digital world fragments this common ground. No two students' search results are identical; no two feeds display the same content. Knowledge becomes personalised, privatised, and often polarised. While this individualisation has benefits—tailoring content to interests can motivate learners—it undermines the possibility of collective understanding. *If literacy once united citizens through shared texts, algorithmic curation risks dividing them through customised realities.*

Yet the algorithmic trap is not inescapable. Awareness is the first line of defence. Students who are explicitly taught how search engines rank results, how recommendation systems function, and how algorithms are shaped by commercial incentives are better equipped to resist narrowing. For example, media literacy programmes that require students to compare different search engines or to analyse the structure of a news feed cultivate habits of scepticism. Similarly, exercises in which learners trace the "information journey" of a viral video—asking how it spread, why it was promoted, and whose interests it served—transform passive consumption into active inquiry. *The key insight is that algorithms are not fate; they are design, and design can be interrogated.*

Educators play a crucial role here. Schools that treat digital tools as transparent windows miss the deeper challenge. To prepare students for the digital age is to equip them with the conceptual tools to see technology as constructed, partial, and interest-driven. This does not mean rejecting digital platforms; it means teaching students to use them critically. A student who understands that a YouTube recommendation is not neutral but optimised for engagement has already taken a crucial step towards digital agency. A learner who questions why certain search results appear first, and who deliberately seeks out alternative perspectives, resists the narrowing loop. *The antidote to the algorithmic trap is not abstinence but awareness, not withdrawal but critical literacy.*

There is a final paradox worth noting. Algorithms have the capacity not only to narrow but to expand, depending on how they are designed and used. Platforms could be configured to deliberately introduce diversity, to recommend content that challenges rather than merely affirms, to expose learners to perspectives they might not otherwise encounter. Some experimental educational systems already attempt this, using algorithmic nudges to broaden rather than constrict. But such approaches run against the grain of commercial logic, where engagement and profit remain the dominant imperatives. Until these incentives shift, the responsibility to resist the algorithmic trap will fall largely on educators, families, and learners themselves.

The central challenge of the digital age is not simply information overload but information curation. Algorithms mediate access to knowledge, often invisibly, and in doing so they shape not just what students know but how they come to know it. The risk is that horizons shrink under the guise of infinite choice, that exploration collapses into repetition, and that curiosity is corralled by the quiet power of code. To understand this is to recognise that *digital literacy today is inseparable from algorithmic literacy*. Students who can read, write, and reason critically must also learn to interrogate the unseen systems that feed them their world. Without this awareness, education risks producing not independent thinkers but dependent users, confident in their fluency but blind to its limits. With it, however, learners can transform algorithms from traps into tools—structures to be navigated consciously, questioned intelligently, and used creatively in the service of knowledge rather than its containment.

Critical Thinking in a Copy-Paste Culture

The digital revolution has delivered education an abundance of tools, resources, and opportunities, yet it has also created a subtle erosion of the very habits of mind that learning was once designed to cultivate. Nowhere is this more evident than in the rise of what might be called the copy-paste culture: a world where information is so readily available, and so frictionlessly transferable, that the act of thinking critically, synthesising ideas, and producing original work can feel optional. *Plagiarism, once the deliberate act of borrowing someone else's words, has become in many cases a symptom of structural habits fostered by digital environments in which replication is easier than reflection.*

Students today live in an ecosystem where pre-packaged knowledge is constantly within reach. Online encyclopaedias, essay mills, shared repositories, and now generative AI systems provide a near-instant shortcut to completed work. The temptation is clear: why wrestle with an argument when you can download one? Why struggle with articulating your own thoughts when a search engine will produce thousands of polished examples in seconds? Yet this shortcut culture is more than an academic integrity problem; it reshapes how students conceive of learning itself. The risk is not only dishonesty but dependency: young people who have never been required to struggle with complex texts, who have never learned to test ideas against counter-arguments, begin to equate learning with the effortless retrieval of answers. *The price of ease is the decline of depth.*

One striking example comes from international surveys of student behaviour, which show that while access to digital resources has skyrocketed, measures of original problem-solving, critical reasoning, and sustained attention have not kept pace. Teachers in secondary and higher education often report a paradoxical pattern: students appear digitally confident, yet their written work frequently reveals shallow engagement. Essays are assembled like patchworks of unattributed quotations, and research projects often replicate surface-level information without any discernible voice or analysis. *The craft of learning—slowing down, questioning, wrestling with complexity—is quietly displaced by the culture of speed and compilation.*

To understand why, one must examine the architecture of digital tools themselves. Platforms are designed to provide instant results, often rewarding the speed of acquisition rather than the quality of reflection. Copying and pasting is not an aberration in such systems but their logical extension. Even well-meaning digital learning environments sometimes prioritise completion metrics and gamified progress over sustained inquiry. In this sense, plagiarism is less an isolated transgression than a symptom of an ecosystem optimised for shortcuts. The moralistic framing of plagiarism as simple dishonesty misses the larger point: *when tools constantly signal that answers matter more than questions, it is hardly surprising that students choose replication over reflection.*

Yet shortcut culture is not confined to formal plagiarism. It manifests in everyday habits of mind: relying on summaries rather than reading original texts, scanning headlines instead of analysing articles, substituting ready-made slides or templates for self-crafted expression. These practices can save time but at a hidden cost. The mental muscles required for critical engagement—comparison, evaluation, synthesis, creative recombination—atrophy when they are not exercised. It is no coincidence that educators increasingly lament students' difficulty with extended writing or independent argumentation. *If the culture of learning rewards shortcuts, then critical thinking becomes a casualty.*

Contrasting perspectives, however, are worth considering. Some argue that copy-paste practices can serve as entry points to knowledge. Remixing, adaptation, and creative re-use are, after all, integral to digital culture. A meme draws its power from replication and transformation; open-source coding communities thrive on copying and modifying existing scripts. From this vantage, the act of borrowing is not inherently antithetical to learning but can be reframed as part of a broader pedagogy of collaboration and co-creation. The crucial distinction lies in intention: is the learner using replication to bypass thought, or to deepen it? *Copying can be an act of avoidance or a stage in the process of mastery, depending on whether it is followed by reflection, critique, and transformation.*

Educational contexts that succeed in resisting shortcut culture tend to make thinking visible and indispensable. For instance, project-based learning environments often require students to demonstrate not only final outputs but the reasoning that led to them—annotated drafts, iterative feedback, reflective commentaries. By emphasising process over product, these models undercut the appeal of copy-paste shortcuts. Similarly, classrooms that incorporate explicit digital literacy instruction—teaching students how to evaluate sources, how to paraphrase responsibly, how to engage with others' ideas ethically—help cultivate discernment rather than dependency. *The antidote to copy-paste culture is not prohibition but pedagogy: the deliberate cultivation of habits that make critical thinking unavoidable.*

Technology itself is not the villain. It can, when used deliberately, reinforce deeper learning habits. Digital annotation tools allow students to engage with texts actively rather than passively. Collaborative platforms can foster peer-to-peer critique and synthesis. Even generative AI, often decried as a plagiarism machine, can be re-purposed into a tool for critical engagement if students are taught to interrogate its outputs, test its reliability, and use it as a springboard for their own analysis. *The line between erosion and enrichment lies not in the technology but in the expectations and structures that guide its use.*

The broader cultural context must also be acknowledged. Students inhabit a world in which speed and efficiency are
where productivity metrics often overshadow depth.
lue adaptability and rapid information retrieval;
themselves by measurable outputs; social
nstantaneous commentary over considered
his backdrop, shortcut culture reflects not

only individual choices but systemic pressures. If society constantly signals that faster is better, it is naïve to expect students to resist shortcuts without explicit counter-training. *Critical thinking in the copy-paste culture is not just an academic requirement but a countercultural stance—an insistence that some forms of depth cannot be rushed.*

The philosophical stakes are significant. Education has always been about more than acquiring facts; it has been about cultivating judgement, discernment, and intellectual independence. When learning is reduced to the retrieval and replication of information, students may gain speed but lose autonomy. They risk becoming users rather than thinkers, compilers rather than critics. The copy-paste culture, left unchecked, produces graduates who can assemble answers but cannot question premises, who can present information but cannot generate insight. *In a society saturated with information, the true scarcity is not knowledge but wisdom—the capacity to think critically amidst abundance.*

To restore critical thinking as the centrepiece of education, systems must resist the seduction of ease. This means designing tasks that cannot be meaningfully outsourced to copy-paste habits, valuing processes of reasoning as much as final products, and modelling in classrooms the patience required for authentic thought. It means acknowledging that plagiarism is not just an act of dishonesty but a symptom of an ecosystem that too often rewards replication over reflection. And it means cultivating in students the confidence that their own thinking, however imperfect, has value. *The most profound lesson in resisting shortcut culture is that thought cannot be downloaded—it must be lived, wrestled with, and earned.*

The Literacy Hierarchy

The assumption that all students who can read and write are equally prepared for the demands of the digital age dangerously misleading. Literacy is not a flat achievement, a threshold crossed once and for all; it is a hierarchy of capabilities, each level offering greater autonomy, discernment, and opportunity. At the base are those who can consume digital content but little more. Higher up are those who can evaluate, contextualise, and question what they encounter. At the summit are creators—individuals who not only navigate information but also produce it responsibly, critically, and with an understanding of its wider impact. *The key determinant of where a student finds themselves on this hierarchy is not exposure to devices but guided practice: the deliberate cultivation of digital discernment through structured support from teachers, parents, and communities.*

This hierarchy matters because the digital world rewards depth of literacy unevenly. A child who merely scrolls through feeds can access entertainment and superficial information but struggles to progress academically or professionally. Another child, encouraged to question, compare, and reflect, develops habits of critical inquiry that serve as scaffolding for higher learning. And a third, guided to create—whether through writing, coding, video production, or collaborative projects—acquires both technical fluency and the confidence to shape discourse rather than passively absorb it. *The divergence is not abstract; it manifests in grades, employability, and civic participation. Those who climb higher in the literacy hierarchy secure long-term advantages that compound over time.*

Educational research underscores this. Studies of information literacy among university students consistently show wide gaps not in basic reading comprehension but in the ability to evaluate online sources. One group accepts the first results provided by search engines, another probes credibility, and a third triangulates information across diverse platforms. The differences in academic performance between these groups are substantial. Those at the top not only produce better essays and projects but demonstrate resilience in adapting to new technologies and contexts. The hierarchy is not simply about skills but about dispositions: curiosity, scepticism, and agency. *What separates one student from another is not whether they can operate a device, but whether they can interrogate and shape the knowledge it delivers.*

Real-world examples illustrate how guided practice shapes outcomes. In Singapore, where digital literacy has been systematically integrated into curricula, students are explicitly trained to question online information, to distinguish advertising from journalism, and to consider the ethics of digital creation. This intentional scaffolding moves learners beyond passive consumption and into higher tiers of the hierarchy. By contrast, in school systems where devices are introduced without corresponding literacy education, students often plateau at surface engagement. They appear competent—able to click, scroll, and submit assignments—but lack the deeper habits that translate into long-term capability. *Without structured guidance, the digital divide is not only about access to technology but about access to the higher rungs of literacy.*

The workplace reveals similar patterns. Employers increasingly note that new graduates, while comfortable with digital platforms, often lack the capacity to evaluate information critically or to generate content that demonstrates originality and credibility. Those who have had guided practice in digital discernment stand out. They can identify misinformation, communicate effectively across media, and adapt to shifting technological landscapes. Over a career, these abilities translate into leadership opportunities, creative problem-solving roles, and the capacity to innovate. Conversely, those stranded on lower rungs may remain dependent users, confined to repetitive or automated tasks. *In the economy of the future, literacy hierarchies will translate directly into professional hierarchies.*

The civic implications are equally stark. Democracies depend on citizens who can distinguish truth from manipulation, evidence from rhetoric, and informed argument from misinformation. Students trained to ask, "Who produced this content? For what purpose? What evidence supports it?" grow into adults capable of resisting propaganda and participating in informed debate. Those without such practice are more susceptible to algorithmically amplified falsehoods and polarising narratives. The literacy hierarchy, then, is not only a matter of personal advancement but of collective resilience. *A society's ability to sustain critical public discourse depends on how many of its members are guided beyond the lower rungs of literacy.*

Critically, the climb up the hierarchy does not happen spontaneously. Comfort with technology is not the same as competence in its use. Left unguided, students often remain at the base, mistaking familiarity for expertise. It is structured practice—teachers modelling evaluation, parents setting expectations for digital engagement, mentors encouraging creation—that enables students to ascend. Case studies from community-based initiatives reveal that when young people are given structured opportunities to create digital content and reflect on its impact, their engagement with information shifts. They begin to see themselves not as passive recipients but as active participants. *Climbing the literacy hierarchy is less about innate aptitude and more about deliberate cultivation.*

At the same time, this hierarchy raises questions of equity. Access to guided practice is uneven. Affluent families may enrol children in coding camps, provide them with opportunities to publish or produce, and model critical digital engagement. Disadvantaged students may lack not only the devices but also the mentorship that enables discernment. Schools in under-resourced areas often struggle to move beyond basic digital training. The result is a compounding cycle: those already advantaged climb higher, while those left behind find the gap widening over time. *Digital literacy is not merely an individual skill but a social inheritance, passed more easily to those already equipped with cultural and economic capital.*

This makes the role of education systems pivotal. Schools that treat literacy as a hierarchy rather than a flat competency are better able to prepare students for the demands of the future. Curricula must be designed not only to teach reading and writing but to embed digital evaluation, ethical creation, and critical reflection. Assessment systems must move beyond measuring surface knowledge to valuing discernment and originality. Teachers must be supported with training and resources that enable them to guide students deliberately up the hierarchy. And policies must recognise that providing devices is insufficient without the scaffolding that turns access into agency. *The literacy hierarchy is not an abstract concept; it is a roadmap for designing education that equips students to thrive rather than merely survive in the digital age.*

Philosophically, the concept of a literacy hierarchy challenges the very idea of equality in education. Equality suggests giving every student the same resources. Equity recognises that some require more support to climb further. In digital literacy, this means recognising that mere access to devices does not place all learners on the same footing. Some will remain confined to consumption unless deliberately guided to critique and create. Others, given mentorship and opportunity, will rise to mastery. The task of educators and policymakers is not only to provide access but to engineer pathways upwards. *What is at stake is not just fairness but the distribution of agency in society.*

To grasp the significance of the literacy hierarchy is to understand that education in the digital age is not about ticking boxes of competence but about cultivating ascending capacities. Each rung matters, but the difference between staying at the base and climbing higher is transformative. Students who learn discernment gain more than grades; they acquire habits of mind that endure across academic, professional, and civic life. They become capable not only of navigating information but of interrogating it, reshaping it, and contributing to it. *The literacy hierarchy is thus not only an educational framework but a vision of human development in a world where information is abundant but wisdom is scarce.*

Chapter 4
The Teacher's Dilemma

Few professions have faced such rapid upheaval in so short a span of time as teaching. Over the past two decades, educators have been handed a succession of technologies—interactive whiteboards, learning management systems, digital assessments, video platforms, adaptive software, and most recently artificial intelligence—each heralded as the next great leap forward for learning. Yet while these tools proliferated, the structures meant to support teachers in integrating them meaningfully lagged far behind. Teachers, the supposed linchpins of the digital revolution in education, often find themselves navigating uncharted waters without maps, training, or even time to reflect. The dilemma is stark: they are expected to harness the transformative potential of technology while simultaneously managing the risks of distraction, inequity, and superficiality. For many, this tension defines their daily practice. *The promise of digital tools collides with the realities of overstretched classrooms, uneven resources, and systemic underinvestment in professional development.*

At the heart of the dilemma lies a deceptively simple question: is technology a tool or a crutch? Used well, digital platforms can enrich learning, opening up possibilities for collaboration, creativity, and personalised instruction. They can help students visualise abstract concepts, engage in authentic inquiry, and access resources that transcend the classroom. Yet used poorly, they risk narrowing learning to multiple-choice quizzes, replacing dialogue with dashboards, and reducing teaching to the management of screens. Teachers who embrace technology without critical discernment may inadvertently cede their professional expertise to software. Those who resist may feel labelled as outdated, struggling against institutional pressures to adopt tools they suspect may hinder rather than help. *The boundary between tool and crutch is not defined by the technology itself but by the pedagogical imagination and support available to those expected to use it.*

The unevenness of this support creates profound disparities. Some teachers are given ongoing training, collaborative opportunities to experiment, and the freedom to adapt tools to their students' needs. Others receive only a brief introduction—perhaps a single afternoon workshop—before being expected to incorporate complex systems into their practice. The result is a professional development gap that mirrors the digital divides students face. In some classrooms, technology enables deep, project-based learning. In others, it becomes a blunt instrument for compliance and test preparation. Research consistently shows that technology alone does not improve outcomes; it is the teacher's capacity to integrate it thoughtfully that makes the difference. But capacity does not arise spontaneously. It requires time, training, and institutional recognition of teaching as a complex, adaptive craft. *When professional development is treated as an afterthought, the result is not digital innovation but digital disillusionment.*

Global case studies reveal this dynamic vividly. In Finland, teachers are trusted as professionals and given autonomy to experiment with digital pedagogy, leading to innovative uses of technology that enhance student agency. By contrast, in parts of the United States and the United Kingdom, teachers report being overwhelmed by top-down mandates to adopt platforms without adequate preparation, leading to frustration and burnout. In Kenya and India, teachers involved in donor-funded tablet initiatives have described both the excitement of new possibilities and the exhaustion of being expected to master unfamiliar systems without consistent support. Some adapt creatively, blending local pedagogical traditions with digital tools. Others quietly set the devices aside, reverting to methods they trust. These stories matter because they show that technology in education is not a universal experience but a situated one: its value depends as much on institutional culture and teacher preparation as on the sophistication of the hardware or software itself. *The most powerful technologies succeed not by replacing teachers but by empowering them to do what they do best: guide, inspire, and challenge learners.*

Underlying the teacher's dilemma is a broader philosophical question: what do we believe education is for? If the goal is efficiency—delivering content quickly, standardising assessment, and producing measurable outcomes—then technology often aligns neatly with institutional priorities. Dashboards track progress, algorithms recommend next steps, and data points accumulate. But if the goal is to cultivate curiosity, resilience, and critical thinking, the reliance on technology as a crutch can be corrosive. Teachers are caught between these competing visions, expected to satisfy accountability systems while also nurturing deeper forms of learning that resist quantification. *Their dilemma is not only technical but moral: how to safeguard the humanity of education in a system increasingly seduced by metrics and machines.*

The chapter that follows examines these tensions with nuance. It will explore how teachers around the world are negotiating the uncharted territory of digital adoption, balancing the promise of new tools against the risk of reducing education to screen management. It will probe the line between technology as tool and technology as crutch, offering insights into how that boundary can be navigated thoughtfully. It will analyse the professional development gap, showing how unequal training perpetuates unequal outcomes for both teachers and students. And it will bring to life stories from classrooms—moments of frustration, innovation, resistance, and transformation—that illustrate the human side of the digital revolution in education. *For in the end, the story of technology in schools is not about the devices themselves but about the teachers who decide, every day, whether they will use them to deepen learning or diminish it.*

Educators in Uncharted Territory

The rapid adoption of digital technologies in schools has transformed expectations of teaching at a pace that far outstrips the capacity of most systems to prepare teachers for the task. Interactive whiteboards arrived before comprehensive training on how to integrate them. Learning management systems were mandated with minimal guidance on effective pedagogy. Tablets and laptops were rolled out en masse without a roadmap for aligning them to curricular goals. More recently, artificial intelligence has entered classrooms through generative writing tools and adaptive software, often before educators have had a chance to grapple with their ethical, cognitive, and cultural implications. Teachers, more than any other group, are being asked to mediate these changes while still fulfilling the traditional expectations of their profession: to deliver knowledge, assess performance, nurture critical thought, and safeguard the social and emotional well-being of their pupils. *The digital transformation of education has placed teachers on the frontline of an experiment whose rules are still being written, yet they are frequently the least supported actors within it.*

Consider the dissonance between adoption and preparation. A school district in the United States may purchase thousands of tablets under pressure from policymakers eager to demonstrate innovation, only to allocate a single day of training before expecting teachers to integrate them into lessons. In the United Kingdom, teachers report being handed new digital assessment platforms alongside directives to "embed them seamlessly," despite having no prior experience with the software and little clarity on how it aligns with existing curricular standards. Across parts of sub-Saharan Africa and South Asia, donor-funded programmes distribute hardware in bulk but neglect to provide the sustained professional development required for teachers to meaningfully adapt their pedagogy. The consequence is not empowerment but anxiety. Many educators feel they are constantly on the back foot, struggling to keep pace with technologies that change faster than the training designed to support them. *It is not the presence of technology itself that destabilises teaching but the lack of coherent, sustained investment in equipping educators to use it purposefully.*

This struggle is compounded by the structural realities of teaching. The profession is already burdened with heavy workloads, accountability pressures, and societal expectations that often extend well beyond academics. To add new layers of digital integration without simultaneously reducing other responsibilities or providing adequate support creates a sense of overload. Teachers are expected to master not only content and pedagogy but also a growing array of technical skills, from troubleshooting devices to navigating complex software dashboards. For some, the digital shift offers opportunities to reimagine practice; for others, it feels like yet another demand in an already untenable workload. The metaphor of "uncharted territory" is apt: teachers are explorers sent to map a new landscape without compasses, provisions, or rest. *What is framed as innovation can, in practice, feel like disorientation.*

There are stark variations in how teachers respond. In contexts where professional trust and structured development are prioritised, teachers often display remarkable ingenuity. Finland, for instance, invests in sustained, research-informed professional learning that enables educators to experiment with digital tools in ways that enhance collaboration and inquiry. Here, teachers feel ownership over the process of integration, leading to thoughtful, context-sensitive innovations. By contrast, in education systems driven by rigid accountability metrics, digital tools are often reduced to compliance mechanisms—software that tracks attendance, measures test readiness, or monitors engagement. Teachers in such systems may feel their role is shrinking, their expertise sidelined by dashboards and data. *Whether teachers thrive or falter in uncharted territory depends less on their personal resilience than on the ecosystems of trust, support, and training within which they work.*

The challenge is not simply technical but philosophical. Education is never neutral; it reflects deeper values about what societies prioritise. When digital adoption is pursued as a symbol of progress, teachers may be pressured to adopt tools for the sake of optics rather than learning. When efficiency is prized, digital systems are designed to streamline data collection rather than deepen understanding. Teachers are left to reconcile these external imperatives with their professional commitment to fostering curiosity, dialogue, and critical engagement. They face an implicit question: should they bend their practice to the shape of the tool, or bend the tool to the needs of their practice? The answer is rarely straightforward, and in the absence of guidance, teachers make ad hoc decisions with long-term implications for student learning. *The lack of coherent vision leaves educators caught between competing logics: technology as solutionism versus education as human development.*

Stories from classrooms around the world illustrate these tensions vividly. In Brazil, one teacher described how a tablet programme initially felt like an imposition, yet through collaboration with colleagues she discovered ways to use the devices for student-led inquiry projects, transforming them from distractions into platforms for creativity. In India, another teacher recounted abandoning a donor-funded digital tool after weeks of frustration when neither training nor technical support was available, concluding that the technology was a burden rather than a benefit. In the United States, during the pandemic, teachers who had once been hesitant about technology became adept at using video conferencing and collaborative platforms out of necessity, but many expressed exhaustion at the lack of institutional recognition for the new labour this demanded. These accounts are not simply anecdotes but indicators of a broader reality: without systemic alignment, digital adoption creates uneven, unpredictable outcomes. *The capacity of teachers to innovate is real, but it cannot substitute for structures that provide consistent, equitable support.*

One of the most overlooked dimensions of this uncharted territory is emotional. Teachers describe feelings of inadequacy when students appear more adept with devices than they are, even though students' fluency is often superficial. They experience frustration when required to implement tools that conflict with their pedagogical instincts. They report fatigue at the constant churn of platforms—learning one system only to see it replaced within a few years. These emotional burdens matter, not only because they affect teacher well-being but because they shape the quality of instruction. A teacher who feels confident, supported, and trusted is more likely to take risks and innovate. A teacher who feels undermined or overwhelmed is more likely to retreat, either by minimising the use of technology or by relying on it mechanically. *The human experience of teachers in this digital shift is as important as the technical affordances of the tools themselves.*

If there is one consistent thread across these diverse experiences, it is that teachers are being asked to lead change without being adequately prepared or supported to do so. They are pioneers without maps, tasked with constructing a pedagogy of the digital age in real time. Some rise to the challenge, creating models of practice that inspire; others withdraw in frustration or burnout. But the common denominator is systemic neglect of their central role. Policy initiatives celebrate devices and platforms while underinvesting in the professional development that would enable teachers to use them wisely. Schools trumpet innovation while overlooking the day-to-day realities of implementation. And societies demand that teachers prepare students for a digital future while giving them neither the tools nor the time to prepare themselves. *The contradiction is unsustainable: to expect teachers to transform education without first transforming the support structures around them is to ask the impossible.*

To understand educators in uncharted territory is to recognise that the future of digital learning hinges not on the sophistication of the tools but on the preparedness of those who wield them. Teachers are not obstacles to innovation but the agents through whom it becomes meaningful. When training, resources, and professional trust are aligned, they can chart paths that enrich learning and expand opportunity. When these supports are absent, technology becomes not an engine of progress but another layer of inequality. *The story of teachers in the digital age is not about their reluctance but about the systemic failures that leave them to navigate the unknown alone.*

Tech as Tool vs. Tech as Crutch

The story of technology in education has always been one of promise entangled with peril. Few dispute that digital tools can enrich classrooms, but the decisive factor lies not in their presence but in their use. A laptop in the hands of a curious student, guided by a thoughtful teacher, can unlock worlds of information and stimulate critical thought. The same laptop, used only to complete automated drills or to passively consume content, risks reducing learning to mechanical compliance. The line between technology as a tool and technology as a crutch is thin, yet the distinction is vital. *When technology deepens engagement, it empowers; when it substitutes for authentic instruction, it diminishes both teachers and students.*

At its best, technology extends human capacity. A carefully designed simulation in physics can allow students to experiment with forces and motion in ways impossible within the confines of a traditional classroom. A collaborative platform can connect learners across geographies, enabling them to co-author projects or exchange cultural perspectives. Assistive technologies can transform accessibility, giving students with disabilities opportunities for participation that were once denied. These uses position technology as a bridge—augmenting the teacher's role, enriching the curriculum, and scaffolding deeper learning. Crucially, they respect the teacher's expertise and amplify the learner's agency. Here, technology is a partner, not a replacement.

Yet in too many contexts, the opposite occurs. Strained by large class sizes, pressured by high-stakes testing, or constrained by limited professional development, schools often reach for digital solutions that prioritise efficiency over enrichment. Software packages are installed that drill students endlessly on multiple-choice questions. Tablets are programmed with pre-packaged lessons that march students through content regardless of pace or prior knowledge. Automated grading systems reduce complex demonstrations of understanding to crude metrics. In these cases, technology functions less as a tool than as a crutch—compensating for systemic inadequacies by narrowing learning to what machines can easily deliver and measure. *Instead of liberating teachers and learners, such uses tether them to the lowest common denominator of educational outcomes.*

The attraction of technology-as-crutch lies in its apparent simplicity. For overburdened teachers, automated marking tools seem to lighten workloads. For policymakers under pressure to demonstrate results, dashboard analytics provide tidy numbers to present to stakeholders. For school leaders with scarce resources, digital packages promise scalability at low cost. But the convenience masks deeper risks. Students trained on repetitive drill-based platforms may achieve short-term gains in test performance while losing the capacity for critical analysis, creativity, or sustained inquiry. Teachers who rely heavily on scripted digital lessons may cede their professional judgement, narrowing their role to classroom management rather than intellectual guidance. *The very efficiencies that make technology appealing can hollow out the human dimensions of education if not carefully balanced.*

This distinction between tool and crutch has historical echoes. When calculators entered mathematics classrooms, educators debated whether they enhanced or eroded numeracy. Those who treated calculators as a crutch allowed students to bypass foundational skills, producing learners adept at pushing buttons but weak in reasoning. Those who framed calculators as tools used them to offload routine calculations, freeing time for higher-order problem-solving. The lesson is clear: technology's educational value is not inherent but contingent on pedagogy. The same holds true for modern digital tools. A search engine can enable expansive research or reduce inquiry to the first result clicked. A learning app can inspire practice or reinforce rote repetition. *The determining variable is not the sophistication of the tool but the intentionality of its use.*

Case studies underscore this duality. In Singapore, where professional development is closely integrated with digital adoption, teachers use technology to foster inquiry-based learning. Students might design experiments, present findings through multimedia, and engage in peer review using digital platforms—technology as catalyst for deeper understanding. By contrast, in some underfunded districts in the United States, tablets are used primarily to administer standardised test preparation modules, reducing student interaction to screen time and isolating learning from creativity or collaboration. Similarly, in parts of sub-Saharan Africa, donor-driven laptop initiatives often prioritised distribution over pedagogical support. Devices became expensive ornaments in classrooms lacking reliable electricity or trained teachers, symbolising technology as crutch for policy ambitions rather than tool for educational growth. *The same devices, when embedded in different ecosystems, yield radically different outcomes.*

The risk of leaning on technology as a crutch is compounded by the subtle erosion of teacher authority. When digital platforms dictate the sequencing of lessons or determine assessment criteria, teachers may feel compelled to conform, even when their professional instincts suggest otherwise. The promise of "personalised learning" can quickly morph into a rigid pathway designed by algorithms rather than by educators who know their students' unique needs. This inversion shifts teachers from designers of learning experiences to overseers of pre-programmed content. Students, in turn, lose the chance to witness intellectual modelling—the ways in which teachers think aloud, pose questions, and navigate ambiguity. *What is lost is not just instructional quality but the human dimension of education: the shared journey of inquiry between teacher and student.*

The danger is not confined to classrooms alone but extends to cultural expectations. Parents, reassured by glossy marketing, may equate screen time with learning without interrogating what that screen time entails. Policymakers, dazzled by innovation rhetoric, may assume that technology itself guarantees progress. EdTech companies, motivated by profit, may promote platforms that prioritise engagement metrics over educational substance. In such a climate, it becomes easy to normalise technology as a crutch—to conflate exposure with enrichment, activity with learning, data with knowledge. *The cultural momentum behind digital adoption can obscure the essential question: does this technology deepen understanding, or merely replace authentic teaching with a digital facsimile?*

None of this is to suggest that technology's role should be diminished. On the contrary, the digital landscape offers unprecedented opportunities for creativity, access, and collaboration. The challenge is to cultivate discernment about how technology is positioned within pedagogy. A thoughtful teacher can transform even basic tools into vehicles of inquiry; an ill-conceived policy can reduce advanced systems to mere compliance mechanisms. The crux of the matter is not whether schools should embrace technology but whether they can resist the temptation to use it as a shortcut. *True innovation lies not in substituting screens for teachers but in designing ecosystems where technology amplifies the uniquely human capacities of curiosity, dialogue, and mentorship.*

Ultimately, distinguishing between tool and crutch requires a shift in perspective. Technology should not be judged solely by its functionality but by the quality of learning it engenders. Does it encourage exploration, foster collaboration, and develop critical faculties? Or does it narrow learning to tasks that machines can easily manage? Does it respect teachers as professionals, or does it reduce them to facilitators of pre-packaged scripts? These questions demand constant vigilance because the line between enrichment and impoverishment is often subtle, shifting with context, training, and intention. *The danger is not that technology will dominate education but that it will quietly reconfigure it into something narrower, more standardised, and less human if we fail to distinguish wisely between when it is a tool and when it is merely a crutch.*

The Professional Development Gap

The assumption that technology alone will transform education is quietly undermined by an uncomfortable reality: teachers are rarely equipped with the training necessary to make meaningful use of digital tools. While governments and school systems often invest heavily in devices, platforms, and infrastructure, far less attention is devoted to the professional development required to integrate these innovations into pedagogy. The result is a widening chasm between the promise of educational technology and its actual impact on learning outcomes. *When training is uneven, outcomes are uneven. The potential of digital learning becomes contingent not on access to hardware but on the degree to which teachers are supported to wield it effectively.*

The problem begins with the pace of technological change. Teachers who trained in the 1990s or early 2000s were prepared for classrooms that bore little resemblance to those of today. They were not instructed in how to facilitate online collaboration, manage blended learning environments, or teach digital literacy. Even newly qualified teachers frequently report that their training did not provide more than a cursory introduction to educational technologies. Instead, they are expected to learn "on the job," often through trial and error, while simultaneously navigating existing curricular demands. In this environment, the unevenness of professional development is both predictable and damaging: some educators become innovators, while others struggle, leaving students' opportunities largely dependent on the luck of their classroom assignment.

The consequences are vividly illustrated in international comparisons. In Finland, where professional development is continuous, collaborative, and well-funded, teachers are encouraged to explore new digital strategies with the confidence that failure is part of the process of innovation. Technology becomes an ally in creative pedagogy because teachers are trusted and supported as professionals. By contrast, in many low- and middle-income countries, devices are introduced without corresponding investment in teacher training. A 1-to-1 laptop initiative may make headlines, but without guidance on lesson design, classroom management, and assessment, laptops are reduced to expensive distractions or, worse, monuments to wasted opportunity. *The gap is not just between schools with technology and those without; it is between teachers who are empowered to use technology thoughtfully and those left to flounder without adequate preparation.*

The unevenness is compounded by systemic inequities. Teachers in affluent schools are more likely to access regular workshops, peer mentoring, and structured professional learning communities. They are given time and resources to experiment with digital tools, to share practices, and to reflect critically on successes and failures. By contrast, teachers in underfunded schools—often those serving the students who could benefit most from high-quality digital integration—are given little more than basic orientation sessions, if that. Professional development is sometimes outsourced to vendors whose primary interest lies in promoting their own products rather than cultivating sustainable pedagogical practices. The outcome is predictable: *technology amplifies inequality not because of its intrinsic nature, but because of the uneven support provided to the humans who must make it meaningful in the classroom.*

One of the most significant obstacles to bridging the professional development gap is the persistent misconception that digital fluency among teachers can be assumed rather than cultivated. Just as the "digital native" myth mischaracterises students' proficiency, there is a parallel tendency to assume that teachers—by virtue of using email, smartphones, or administrative platforms—are naturally prepared to integrate sophisticated educational technologies into their practice. This assumption leads to tokenistic workshops that prioritise technical demonstrations over pedagogical integration. A teacher may learn how to log into a platform and assign quizzes but not how to weave that platform into a coherent learning sequence that builds critical thinking, creativity, or collaboration. *Training focused on functionality without pedagogy is training destined to fail.*

There is also a psychological dimension. Many teachers feel a loss of confidence when new technologies are introduced, particularly when professional development is insufficient or rushed. For some, this leads to withdrawal: they stick to traditional methods out of fear of exposing their uncertainty.

For others, it generates resentment, especially when technology is perceived as imposed from above by policymakers or administrators without consultation. In contrast, teachers who are given agency in shaping how digital tools are adopted—who are treated as partners rather than passive implementers—are far more likely to embrace experimentation. The difference is profound: empowerment cultivates ownership, while neglect breeds resistance.

Case studies provide concrete evidence of this dynamic. In Uruguay's Plan Ceibal, one of the earliest large-scale laptop distribution programmes, the government initially underestimated the importance of teacher training. Early evaluations found that while devices were widely distributed, their educational use was limited. Recognising this, Uruguay later invested heavily in professional development, creating support networks, peer collaboration, and ongoing mentoring. The programme's effectiveness improved markedly once teachers were no longer left to figure things out alone. Contrast this with initiatives in parts of sub-Saharan Africa, where donor-funded laptops were introduced without systematic training. Devices languished unused in cupboards or were employed solely for typing practice because teachers had no framework for integrating them into meaningful learning experiences. *Technology alone did not fail—what failed was the absence of human support to animate its potential.*

Even in wealthier contexts, gaps persist. In the United States, professional development often varies dramatically not only between districts but within them. One school may have instructional technology coaches who co-teach lessons and mentor staff, while another in the same district relies on occasional after-school workshops with poor attendance. This patchwork approach ensures that adoption is inconsistent, reinforcing inequities between schools and even between classrooms. Meanwhile, in East Asian contexts such as South Korea, where systemic investment in teacher training is robust, digital learning is more consistently integrated across schools, though even here the pressure of high-stakes examinations can reduce technology to a tool of test preparation rather than creativity. *The lesson across contexts is clear: professional development is the linchpin that determines whether technology narrows or widens educational horizons.*

The deeper philosophical issue is that professional development is too often treated as an afterthought rather than as a central component of educational design. Policymakers celebrate device distribution as a visible metric of progress—photographs of students with new tablets or laptops are easy to showcase. Professional development, by contrast, is less photogenic, more labour-intensive, and more difficult to quantify. Yet it is precisely this invisible investment in human capital that determines the success or failure of digital education initiatives. A system that invests in hardware without investing in teachers is like a hospital purchasing advanced medical equipment without training doctors in its use: the tools become impressive artefacts but fail to improve outcomes.

Closing the professional development gap requires more than offering occasional training sessions. It demands a reorientation of priorities: sustained, collaborative, and context-sensitive support must become the norm rather than the exception. Teachers need time built into their schedules for reflection and experimentation, not simply add-on workshops layered onto already overloaded calendars. They need professional learning communities where they can exchange insights and adapt strategies to local needs. They need mentoring and coaching models that emphasise pedagogy first, tools second. They need assurance that innovation is valued over perfection, that the goal is not flawless adoption but thoughtful integration. *Without these supports, the promise of technology will continue to outpace the reality of classroom practice.*

Ultimately, the professional development gap is not just about skill but about justice. Uneven training perpetuates uneven outcomes, ensuring that the students who most need transformative teaching are the least likely to receive it. Addressing the gap is therefore not a peripheral concern but a moral imperative. If digital education is to live up to its rhetoric of empowerment and equity, then teachers must be equipped with more than devices—they must be given the sustained professional support that transforms those devices into instruments of genuine learning. The future of digital education depends not on the sophistication of tools but on the wisdom and confidence of the professionals who wield them. *The decisive investment is not in machines but in minds.*

Stories from the Classroom

The fate of digital learning is decided not in policy papers or technology fairs but in the classrooms where teachers stand at the front of their students each day. The glossy rhetoric of innovation meets the realities of pedagogy in spaces where chalk dust still lingers, budgets are stretched thin, and human relationships remain the most decisive factor in whether technology fulfils its promise or deepens frustration. Teachers are not passive implementers of tools designed elsewhere; they are mediators, translators, and, at times, resisters. *The story of digital education is therefore best told through their experiences, for it is in their hands that technology either becomes an instrument of transformation or a burden to be endured.*

One vivid case comes from a secondary school in Nairobi, where a mathematics teacher named Esther initially greeted her school's introduction of tablets with scepticism. The devices arrived with much fanfare, but training was minimal, and many of her colleagues defaulted to using them as glorified digital textbooks. Esther, however, began experimenting with interactive geometry apps, allowing students to manipulate shapes, test theorems, and visualise equations in ways that chalk and board could never offer. She recalls how one student, who had struggled with abstract concepts, suddenly lit up when he could rotate a triangle on the screen and watch the properties unfold before his eyes. The shift was not in the device itself but in Esther's willingness to adapt her pedagogy, to make the abstract tactile. Yet in the same school, other teachers left their tablets locked in cupboards, citing the lack of time and support. *The same tool produced enrichment in one classroom and inertia in another, underscoring the decisive role of the teacher's response.*

In rural America, stories reveal a different tension. A school district in West Virginia invested heavily in laptops for every child, confident that the move would modernise its classrooms. Yet many teachers found themselves struggling with patchy broadband and outdated systems that slowed lessons rather than streamlined them. A history teacher, Jim, described how his students would lose focus while waiting for websites to load, drifting into social media rather than engaging with primary sources. After several years of frustration, he returned to paper-based resources, arguing that the unreliability of the digital infrastructure eroded rather than enhanced his teaching. His experience highlights a critical truth: technology introduced without reliable infrastructure risks not only inefficiency but also a collapse of trust in the very idea of digital learning. *When teachers are forced into constant firefighting with technology, frustration trumps innovation.*

Contrast this with experiences in Singapore, where systemic investment in both infrastructure and training has allowed teachers to redefine practice on a wide scale. At Raffles Institution, science teachers use data-logging tools and cloud-based simulations to allow students to design and test experiments virtually before conducting them in the lab. Rather than replacing hands-on work, technology augments it by expanding the range of experimentation and accelerating feedback loops. Teachers report that students arrive at physical labs with more refined hypotheses and sharper questions. This is not technology as a shortcut but technology as a scaffold for deeper engagement. Crucially, these successes stem from a system where professional development, peer collaboration, and administrative support are sustained, not sporadic. *Here, digital tools are not an imposition but a carefully integrated extension of pedagogy.*

Another compelling case comes from Brazil, where a government-backed programme aimed to democratise digital access in underfunded schools. In one São Paulo classroom, teacher Mariana integrated digital storytelling projects using tablets. Students from low-income backgrounds created multimedia narratives of their neighbourhoods, combining photos, interviews, and written reflections. The exercise not only honed digital literacy but also cultivated civic awareness, allowing students to see their everyday environments as worthy of critical inquiry. Mariana reflected that for many students, it was the first time they had been asked to frame their experiences as stories with value. Yet in other schools under the same programme, tablets were primarily used for drill-and-practice software designed to prepare students for standardised tests. Teachers there felt pressure from administrators to demonstrate quantifiable improvements in test scores, so they channelled technology into the narrowest of uses. The result was a stark divide: in one setting, technology expanded horizons; in another, it narrowed them further. *The same policy initiative produced radically different educational landscapes depending on how teachers were empowered to interpret it.*

Teachers' frustrations are not always born of incompetence but of conflicting demands. In London, an English teacher named David described how his school adopted a new learning management system that was supposed to streamline assignment submissions and feedback. Instead, the system doubled his workload, requiring him to input data in multiple formats for reporting purposes. He found himself spending evenings navigating poorly designed interfaces rather than crafting meaningful feedback for students. After several months, he reverted to handwritten comments on essays, arguing that no amount of digital sheen could justify sacrificing the relational core of his teaching. His story illustrates the danger of mistaking administrative efficiency for pedagogical gain. *When technology prioritises data extraction over learning, teachers often disengage, not because they resist change but because they protect what matters most.*

Stories from classrooms also reveal resilience and creativity. In India, where large class sizes and resource shortages are common, a teacher named Anil used free online platforms to flip his classroom. He recorded short video lessons in Hindi, allowing students to watch explanations at home or in school libraries, and used classroom time for problem-solving and discussion. This hybrid model allowed him to differentiate support for students at different levels, something nearly impossible in a class of sixty. His approach spread informally among colleagues, illustrating how teacher-led innovation can ripple through systems even when official training is absent. Yet Anil also admitted that without stable internet access, some students were excluded, highlighting the persistent infrastructure barrier. *Innovation flourishes when teachers are given agency, but inequities still define who can fully benefit.*

From these stories, one theme emerges: technology itself does not determine outcomes—teachers do. The same tablet can be a window to critical inquiry or a tool of rote repetition. The same platform can amplify creativity or drown teachers in bureaucracy. The difference lies in context, training, support, and, above all, professional agency. Where teachers are trusted, resourced, and given space to experiment, they redefine their practice in ways that enrich learning. Where they are neglected or constrained, frustration leads to abandonment, and the rhetoric of innovation collapses into disillusionment.

These classroom stories matter because they ground the debate on digital learning in lived realities rather than abstract promises. They remind us that education is not transformed by devices alone but by the interplay of human judgement, institutional priorities, and cultural context. *If we are to bridge digital divides, we must first listen to the voices of those who face them daily in classrooms around the world.*

Chapter 5
Culture, Class, and the Digital Divide

The story of digital inequality is often told in the language of infrastructure—of wires, bandwidth, and devices—but to stop there is to miss the deeper terrain in which inequality takes root. Beyond the mechanics of access lies the cultural dimension: the ways in which technology becomes a marker of privilege, a tool of exclusion, and, for some, a lever of mobility. Just as Pierre Bourdieu described cultural capital as the invisible asset that reproduces social hierarchies across generations, *technological fluency now functions as a twenty-first century form of capital, one that is unevenly distributed, subtly inherited, and powerfully determinative of life chances.* This chapter takes us beyond the physical and economic barriers already explored, into the social and cultural patterns that determine not just who uses technology, but how, and to what effect.

Consider a child in a middle-class family in London who has grown up with not only broadband and a personal laptop but also parents who model research strategies, question online claims, and encourage exploratory coding projects. Now compare this with a child of the same age in a low-income household, where a shared device is used mainly for entertainment, data is rationed, and parents, unfamiliar with digital tools, cannot provide meaningful guidance. Both children have "access" in the narrow sense, but one has inherited a form of *technological cultural capital*—ways of using, navigating, and leveraging digital tools that compound advantage over time—while the other has not. The divergence is not rooted in innate ability but in the subtle intergenerational transmission of digital practices, expectations, and literacies. Just as Bourdieu argued that cultural knowledge of art, language, and etiquette distinguished elites from others, today it is the invisible layer of digital competence and discernment that sets trajectories apart.

These disparities become starker when viewed through the lens of the Global North and South. In wealthy nations, the debate often centres on optimising digital use: how to manage screen time, how to balance enrichment with distraction, how to ensure students move from passive consumption to active creation. In much of the Global South, however, the questions are more foundational: how to maintain connectivity during power cuts, how to teach when three siblings share one phone, how to deliver lessons when platforms are available only in English. Technology, far from levelling the playing field, can deepen divides by layering structural inequities over cultural and linguistic barriers. A child in Nairobi who navigates online resources through English, often their third language, faces a different cognitive challenge than a peer in New York whose digital ecosystem is tailored to their mother tongue. *Digital inequality is not a single story; it manifests differently depending on the cultural, linguistic, and economic soil in which technology is planted.*

The dominance of English in online platforms illustrates how language itself has become a gatekeeper of digital capital. The world's largest repositories of knowledge—from Wikipedia to YouTube tutorials—are overwhelmingly produced in English. While translation tools have improved, they often flatten nuance, exclude idiomatic expression, and misrepresent technical precision. Learners in Latin America, South Asia, or Francophone Africa are therefore doubly disadvantaged: first by infrastructure gaps, and second by linguistic ones that render global knowledge less accessible or more cognitively demanding. Meanwhile, those fluent in English acquire not only direct access to content but also the cultural codes and references that circulate within global digital spaces.

Language is not merely a medium of communication; it is a currency of participation in the digital economy.

Within countries themselves, new educational elites are emerging, defined not simply by wealth but by the capacity to convert wealth into digital capital. Affluent families in New Delhi, São Paulo, or Toronto enrol their children in coding academies, pay for personalised online tutoring, or curate carefully selected digital experiences that cultivate creativity and problem-solving skills. They treat technology not as a distraction to be policed but as an asset to be strategically managed. For children in these households, platforms such as Khan Academy or online STEM clubs become springboards into academic excellence and career preparedness. Contrast this with the experience of children in low-income families who might use the same platforms only sporadically, lacking not only the resources for paid upgrades but also the parental scaffolding to sustain disciplined engagement. The digital divide here is not about access to devices but about the *capacity to convert digital access into enduring advantage.*

This dynamic risks normalising a two-tier system in which technology becomes a multiplier of class privilege rather than a bridge across it. Wealthier families are not merely buying faster devices or more reliable broadband; they are purchasing time, attention, and guidance. A private tutor who helps a student navigate online platforms teaches not just the subject matter but the meta-skill of how to learn in digital environments. These are the skills—critical evaluation, productive use of platforms, strategic engagement with algorithms—that accumulate invisibly, shaping future competitiveness in ways that are difficult to quantify but profoundly consequential. *The quiet accumulation of digital cultural capital may prove to be one of the most potent engines of inequality in our time.*

As we enter this chapter, the challenge is clear: to interrogate the cultural dimensions of the digital divide with the same rigour we apply to questions of infrastructure and economics. Technology does not exist in a vacuum; it is mediated by class, by language, by cultural practices, and by inherited patterns of advantage. Understanding these dynamics demands that we resist simplistic narratives of "access for all" and instead grapple with the layered realities that define how digital tools are integrated into lives. For some, technology is a launchpad; for others, a ceiling. For a privileged few, it is a fluent second language; for many, it remains a dialect half-understood. And for educational systems around the world, the central question is whether technology will reproduce hierarchies or disrupt them.

The pages ahead will show that if we are serious about digital equity, we must move beyond the promise of devices and bandwidth to confront the subtler, more entrenched realities of culture and class. It is only by addressing these cultural divides—the inherited habits, the linguistic exclusions, the ways privilege is converted into opportunity—that we can begin to ensure that technology does not simply mirror the inequalities of the offline world but provides a chance, however difficult, to redress them.

Tech as Cultural Capital

The digital age has not erased the social hierarchies of the past; it has translated them into new forms. Where earlier centuries prized mastery of literature, etiquette, or the arts as hallmarks of cultural sophistication, today, *technological fluency has become a defining form of capital.* It is not simply a question of knowing how to operate devices but of understanding how to navigate, adapt, and thrive within digital ecosystems whose logic now governs education, employment, and civic participation. Pierre Bourdieu's concept of cultural capital—those non-financial assets such as knowledge, skills, and dispositions that enable individuals to maintain or improve their social position—offers a powerful lens through which to understand why digital divides persist even when physical access appears universal. For just as with cultural capital, technological fluency is inherited, cultivated, and unevenly distributed.

The evidence is everywhere, though it is often obscured by the comforting myth that younger generations are "digital natives." A teenager scrolling with ease on TikTok may appear fluent, but fluency in the context of cultural capital is not measured by casual consumption. It is measured by the ability to discern credible information from noise, to mobilise platforms strategically for learning or professional advancement, and to create rather than merely consume. These deeper competences do not emerge spontaneously from exposure. They are nurtured through family environments, school practices, and social networks—precisely the pathways through which cultural capital of all forms is transmitted. In affluent households, parents are more likely to guide children toward online resources, scaffold their engagement with digital learning tools, and model habits of critical inquiry. In contrast, families with fewer resources may see devices primarily as tools of entertainment or functional communication, not as gateways to opportunity. Both sets of children have access, but only one set acquires the cultural capital of digital fluency.

This intergenerational transmission is striking when examined in global education systems. In countries such as Finland or Singapore, where schools integrate coding, digital citizenship, and media literacy into mainstream curricula, digital capital is institutionally cultivated and widely distributed. In these contexts, students learn not just how to use tools but how to interrogate them. By contrast, in underfunded systems from rural India to inner-city America, technology integration is often superficial—focused on test preparation apps or low-level skills rather than higher-order literacies. The result is a widening gap: some students are being prepared to shape the digital economy, while others are being prepared merely to function within it. *Technology, far from erasing inequalities, is amplifying them through the mechanism of cultural capital.*

Case studies reveal the subtlety of these divides. A middle-class student in Paris might be encouraged to use online archives to support history essays, to participate in a virtual debate club, or to publish reflections on platforms such as Medium. These practices cultivate both confidence and competence in public digital spaces. A student of the same age in a less advantaged environment may rely on a shared smartphone, downloading offline notes or watching tutorial videos without opportunities for active production or feedback. Both are "online," but only one is accumulating the symbolic and practical capital that carries weight in higher education and professional contexts. Just as familiarity with classical music once signalled belonging in elite circles, so too does fluency in the tools of digital research, coding, or multimedia production mark belonging in today's knowledge economy.

The inheritance of digital capital is not simply about what is taught but also about what is modelled. Children absorb not only skills but attitudes—whether technology is seen as a space for exploration, a source of creativity, or a minefield of risks to be avoided. A parent who confidently navigates e-banking, online health resources, or remote work platforms demonstrates to their child that digital tools are enablers of agency. A parent overwhelmed by updates, fearful of scams, or locked out of essential services may unconsciously pass on a disposition of avoidance or mistrust. *Bourdieu's insight that capital is both material and embodied—that it exists as habitus as much as ascribed knowledge—is especially evident in the digital sphere.*

The role of institutions in legitimising digital capital cannot be understated. Universities increasingly assume baseline fluency in digital research methods, collaborative platforms, and online academic integrity tools. Employers filter applicants by their digital presence, expecting LinkedIn profiles, portfolios, or coding projects as evidence of professional maturity. Those who arrive at these thresholds already equipped with digital cultural capital are advantaged; those who do not face a hidden curriculum of catch-up. This is not merely about skill acquisition but about the social value attributed to certain competences. Knowing how to navigate complex learning management systems or to interpret algorithmic search results signals not just ability but *belonging* within spaces of power and opportunity.

What complicates the picture is that digital cultural capital, unlike traditional cultural markers such as accent or mannerisms, evolves rapidly. The tools that confer advantage today—Python, data visualisation, digital design—may be supplanted tomorrow. This volatility makes the inheritance of dispositions and strategies even more important than the inheritance of specific skills. Those taught to adapt, to self-teach, and to critically assess new tools will continue to accumulate advantage across shifting landscapes. Those trained only in surface-level operations risk obsolescence as platforms evolve. The divide, then, is not just between access and no access but between adaptive fluency and functional stagnation.

Critically, this perspective reframes the debate about digital inequality. Rather than assuming that closing the device gap will produce equity, we must ask: *who has the cultural scaffolding to turn devices into capital?* When coding bootcamps flourish in wealthy urban centres but remain inaccessible in rural districts, when international schools embed digital project work while public schools rely on drill-and-practice software, when wealthier parents pay for online tutors while others ration data, the result is a quiet but profound stratification. Just as Bourdieu described cultural capital as the mechanism through which elites reproduce themselves, so too is technological fluency becoming a mechanism for reproducing digital elites.

This also has global implications. Nations that invest in digital capital for their citizens—through education, language support, and infrastructure—are positioning themselves competitively in the global economy. Those that neglect this dimension risk consigning entire generations to the periphery of digital modernity. Within societies, the stakes are equally high: digital capital shapes not only who thrives in the labour market but also who can participate fully in democratic processes, cultural production, and civic life. The ability to discern misinformation, to mobilise social media effectively, or to leverage open data is no longer a luxury; it is a precondition of informed citizenship.

Seen in this light, technology is not the great equaliser it is often claimed to be. It is a form of symbolic capital, mirroring Bourdieu's original insight: valuable because it is scarce, and scarce because it is embedded in systems of social reproduction. The challenge for educators, policymakers, and families is not merely to expand access but to democratise the practices, dispositions, and literacies that turn access into advantage. Until that happens, the digital world will continue to reflect the inequalities of the physical one, with technological fluency functioning as both a gatekeeper and a passport to opportunity.

The concept of *tech as cultural capital* forces us to confront an uncomfortable truth: the digital divide is not closing as quickly as it appears. It is changing shape, from a visible gap of devices and bandwidth to an invisible hierarchy of literacies, competences, and inherited practices. And because these forms of capital are transmitted subtly—through family conversations, school environments, peer networks—they are harder to detect, harder to measure, and harder to redress. Yet they are also precisely where the battle for equity must be fought. For in a world governed by algorithms, platforms, and networks, the capacity to turn technology into cultural capital is not merely advantageous—it is decisive.

Global South vs. Global North Realities

The story of digital inequality is often told in terms of access: who has devices, who does not; who has broadband, who is left behind. Yet this framing masks the deeper truth that the digital divide is not a single gap but a constellation of disparities shaped by history, geography, culture, and economics. Nowhere is this more evident than in the contrasting realities of the Global South and the Global North. While both regions grapple with challenges of digital integration, the forms these challenges take—and their implications for education and social mobility—are profoundly different. To understand digital inequality, one must look not just at connectivity statistics but at the lived contexts that define what connectivity enables, constrains, and excludes.

A striking paradox emerges when comparing developed and developing contexts. In the Global North, high-speed broadband and near-universal device penetration have become the norm, yet this very ubiquity creates subtler inequalities: differences in digital literacy, cultural capital, and the ways technology is integrated into learning and work. In the Global South, meanwhile, the barriers are often more visible and material. Millions of households lack stable internet connections, rely on shared or outdated devices, or contend with infrastructure so fragile that digital participation is intermittent at best. Here, inequality is not only about what people can *do* online but whether they can be online at all. *The divide, therefore, is not simply quantitative—it is qualitative, shaped by the nature of access and the conditions under which it is exercised.*

Consider rural Kenya, where community-based initiatives have brought tablets into schools through solar-powered charging stations. At first glance, this mirrors one-to-one device programmes in Europe or North America. Yet the educational experience is not equivalent. Students often share devices, lack stable connectivity to access cloud-based resources, and receive little training in how to apply digital tools beyond basic exercises. Contrast this with a secondary school in Denmark, where each student not only has a personal laptop but also engages in structured programmes of digital literacy, data ethics, and coding. Both groups are "connected," yet the opportunities diverge radically. *Connectivity without context is not empowerment; it is exposure without advantage.*

Economic models further complicate the picture. In developed economies, subscription services—whether for educational apps, online courses, or productivity tools—are often framed as incremental expenses layered on top of already robust infrastructure. Families may complain about costs, but participation is generally possible. In many parts of the Global South, however, these subscription models become exclusionary. A family that can afford a single smartphone may still find the recurring data costs prohibitive, forcing children to ration online time or choose between school assignments and social interaction. The supposed democratisation of learning platforms thus reproduces class divisions, with wealthier households able to sustain continuous digital engagement and poorer ones left with fragmented, inconsistent access.

Cultural dynamics are equally important. The dominance of English across global platforms skews the value of digital engagement toward those who are already proficient in the language. For students in Nigeria or Bangladesh, engaging deeply with online resources often requires not only connectivity but also linguistic capital. Meanwhile, digital ecosystems in Europe or North America, while also shaped by linguistic hierarchies, are more closely aligned with users' native tongues. This disparity reinforces global knowledge asymmetries: a physics student in Ghana may need to translate course materials or struggle with subtitled lectures, while her counterpart in Germany can access a wealth of resources seamlessly. *Language is not a side issue of digital inequality—it is a structural barrier that multiplies other disadvantages.*

The Global South also faces systemic challenges in the educational use of technology. Teachers often lack the professional development, curricular resources, or institutional support needed to integrate digital tools effectively. For example, in many Indian public schools, computer labs exist in name but sit unused due to lack of trained staff or maintenance. In contrast, schools in the Global North are more likely to have ongoing professional development, IT support teams, and curricular frameworks that embed technology in pedagogy. This divergence is critical: *technology is not self-executing; its impact depends on the human systems that surround it.*

Yet it would be misleading to frame the Global North as uniformly advantaged and the Global South as uniformly disadvantaged. There are innovative models emerging in the South that highlight resilience and creativity. Mobile-first strategies, such as the widespread use of WhatsApp for educational coordination in Brazil or radio-Internet hybrids in parts of sub-Saharan Africa, demonstrate adaptive uses of limited resources. In some cases, these innovations surpass the rigidity of Northern systems, which can become overly reliant on formal infrastructure. Conversely, pockets of inequality persist in the North: rural America struggles with broadband deserts, and migrant families across Europe face barriers of affordability and digital literacy that echo the challenges of the South. The distinction, then, is not absolute but contextual, with each region facing its own blend of structural and cultural constraints.

Philosophically, the divide speaks to deeper questions of equity and power. If Bourdieu's framework of cultural capital helps us understand intra-societal inequality, then world-systems theory offers a lens for inter-societal digital inequality. Just as the Global North has historically extracted resources from the South, so too does the digital economy risk perpetuating dependency. The North dominates not only in infrastructure but also in platform ownership, algorithm design, and data governance. Students in the South often learn on platforms designed in Silicon Valley, whose assumptions about cultural norms, linguistic access, and user behaviour reflect Northern contexts. *Digital dependence becomes the new face of global dependency, ensuring that even as students in the South gain access, they remain consumers rather than co-creators of digital systems.*

This imbalance carries long-term economic implications. Nations that fail to cultivate digital sovereignty—through local platforms, culturally relevant content, and inclusive infrastructure—risk consigning future generations to peripheral roles in the global economy. Meanwhile, countries that invest strategically in digital education and infrastructure, as seen in Rwanda's ambitious ICT-in-education initiatives or Uruguay's Plan Ceibal, can reposition themselves more competitively. The question is not merely one of catching up but of defining terms of participation. *To be digitally included is not only to be online but to be able to shape the digital world on one's own terms.*

At its heart, the Global South vs. Global North divide underscores a truth often lost in the rhetoric of universal access: digital inequality is not a single problem with a single solution. It is an evolving matrix of economic, cultural, linguistic, and institutional disparities that demand context-sensitive strategies. Where the North grapples with issues of depth—how to cultivate critical digital literacies in saturated environments—the South wrestles with issues of breadth—how to ensure stable, affordable, and meaningful access. Both are forms of inequality, and both carry profound implications for the future of education, citizenship, and global equity.

What becomes clear is that the digital divide is not closing but transforming. The metrics of devices and broadband subscriptions may suggest progress, but the lived realities tell another story: one of stratification, dependency, and unequal opportunity. Understanding these divergent realities is not merely an academic exercise; it is essential for building a digital future that is genuinely inclusive. Without recognising the specific contours of inequality in both the South and the North, we risk perpetuating the illusion of progress while entrenching the very hierarchies we claim to dismantle.

Language and Local Context

Digital technology has often been heralded as the great equaliser, collapsing borders and placing the world's knowledge within reach of anyone with an internet connection. Yet behind this narrative lies a less discussed but equally significant reality: the internet speaks predominantly in English, and this linguistic dominance quietly entrenches inequality in ways that hardware distribution or broadband expansion alone cannot solve. *Access without language is an incomplete form of access; it opens the door but locks the shelves.* For learners navigating ecosystems where English is not the primary medium, the global digital commons remains less a shared library than a gated archive.

The scale of this imbalance is staggering. Estimates suggest that while English is spoken natively by less than 6% of the world's population, more than half of all online content is in English. By contrast, widely spoken languages such as Arabic, Hindi, or Swahili command a fraction of that digital presence. This asymmetry matters because students and educators in non-Anglophone regions are compelled either to work through a second language or to make do with sparse, often outdated resources in their own. The result is that digital inequality is not merely about *whether* one can connect but *what kind* of knowledge one can meaningfully access once connected.

Consider a student in rural Mexico seeking to learn advanced physics. While she may have a device and intermittent connectivity, the vast majority of quality open resources—MIT lectures, academic papers, simulations—are in English. Her grasp of the subject is therefore tethered to her English proficiency, not her intellectual ability. Meanwhile, her peer in Canada encounters no such barrier; fluency in English grants him seamless access to the world's richest academic libraries. The inequality here is not visible in device counts or broadband penetration data, yet it is no less profound. *Language, in the digital age, has become an invisible gatekeeper of opportunity.*

The dominance of English also shapes how knowledge itself is constructed and validated online. Search engines are optimised for English-language queries; algorithms prioritise English-language results; platforms design interfaces around Anglophone cultural norms. A student in Senegal searching for agricultural innovations in Wolof may find only a handful of results, while the same query in English returns thousands of relevant pages. Over time, this dynamic nudges learners toward English not simply as a language but as the assumed "default" of knowledge. The danger is that entire knowledge traditions—oral histories, indigenous sciences, local pedagogies—become marginalised or erased in digital space.

These asymmetries are reinforced by educational policy. In many countries of the Global South, governments promote English-medium instruction precisely because digital resources are overwhelmingly in English. While pragmatic, this shift carries cultural costs: children learn core subjects in a second language, often at the expense of depth and comprehension, and local languages are devalued in both formal education and informal learning. This phenomenon is not limited to Africa or Asia; even in Europe, students from minority language communities such as Basque or Welsh face the same pressure to translate their learning into English in order to access digital materials. *The global dominance of*

English thus shapes not only access but identity, pressuring linguistic minorities to adapt or be excluded.

The educational effects are not uniform. Learners with strong institutional support, such as bilingual programmes or translation tools, can sometimes bridge the gap. Wealthier families may hire private tutors to help children navigate English-heavy platforms or invest in premium tools with localisation options. For poorer households, however, the costs of translation—whether financial, cognitive, or emotional—become yet another layer of disadvantage. Even when machine translation offers partial relief, the quality varies dramatically. Technical subjects, idiomatic expressions, or culturally nuanced concepts often emerge garbled, leaving students to decode not just content but the distortions introduced by imperfect translation.

Case studies illustrate both the problem and emerging solutions. In Ethiopia, the scarcity of Amharic digital resources has historically hindered online learning, but grassroots initiatives such as digital dictionaries and community-based translation collectives are beginning to close the gap. In China, by contrast, the state has invested heavily in creating Mandarin-language platforms, ensuring that learners have access to vast resources without reliance on English. Yet this model, while effective in scale, also raises questions of censorship and state control, showing that localisation alone does not guarantee educational equity. The challenge is not simply creating content in more languages but ensuring that this content is high-quality, independent, and globally connected.

Philosophically, the issue speaks to the relationship between language and power. English has become the lingua franca of digital modernity not by neutral inevitability but by historical and economic dominance. The internet's infrastructure, from coding languages to content platforms, reflects the priorities of English-speaking nations and corporations. To frame this merely as a practical problem of translation misses the deeper point: *when one language dominates, so too does a particular worldview.* Knowledge is not only transmitted but shaped by the language through which it is expressed, meaning that linguistic inequality perpetuates cultural inequality.

The stakes are long-term and structural. Students who can navigate English-dominated platforms accrue advantages that compound over time, translating into better academic outcomes, access to international universities, and participation in the global economy. Those excluded or delayed in this process fall further behind, creating an educational divide that mirrors and reinforces class divides within nations and between them. Unlike infrastructure disparities, which can be addressed with investment in broadband or devices, linguistic divides require subtler, longer-term solutions: investment in translation, the creation of multilingual digital resources, and pedagogical models that value linguistic diversity rather than treating it as an obstacle to overcome.

Some promising experiments suggest a path forward. Collaborative translation projects, such as the localisation of Wikipedia into dozens of underrepresented languages, demonstrate the power of volunteer communities. AI-driven tools hold potential for real-time translation, though they must be developed with sensitivity to context, dialect, and cultural nuance rather than assuming a universal English template. Educational platforms could design with multilingualism at their core rather than as an afterthought, ensuring that learners can access, contribute, and create in their native languages. Such changes require not only technological innovation but also political will, recognising that linguistic equity is a matter of justice as much as pedagogy.

Ultimately, the dominance of English in digital learning environments underscores that technology alone does not level the playing field. Devices and broadband are only part of the story; *language remains the substrate of learning, and unequal linguistic landscapes yield unequal educational futures.* If the goal of digital education is not merely access but empowerment, then multilingualism cannot be peripheral. It must be central to the design of platforms, policies, and pedagogies. Without this, the global classroom risks becoming an echo chamber of English-speaking privilege, where billions are permitted entry but denied full participation.

The New Educational Elites

Education has always been a lever for social stratification, but the digital revolution has widened the gap between those who can afford to weaponise technology as an accelerant and those who can only access it as a baseline. Wealthier families are not merely providing their children with laptops or tablets—they are curating entire digital ecosystems around them. Tutors are available on demand through global platforms, coding academies have replaced the weekend piano lesson, and algorithm-driven personalised learning tools are seamlessly integrated into daily routines. *The result is the quiet construction of a new educational elite—children whose exposure to technology is not only broader but deeper, more strategic, and ultimately more transformative.*

The privilege manifests in multiple layers. At the most visible level, affluent families can purchase access to subscription-based learning platforms that claim to offer adaptive tutoring, gamified maths mastery, or intensive exam preparation. But the advantage does not stop at access; it extends to the ways in which these tools are embedded into broader educational strategies. A child from a high-income household might attend school during the day, then reinforce concepts with a private online tutor in the evening, followed by structured sessions on a coding platform at the weekend. The layering effect creates compounding returns, not unlike financial investment, where early capital multiplies over time. By contrast, a child from a lower-income background may rely on a shared device, sporadic internet, and free resources of uneven quality, with little parental support to scaffold the experience.

The growth of coding academies exemplifies this divergence. In cities from San Francisco to Singapore, children as young as six are being enrolled in after-school coding clubs that treat computational thinking as a core literacy rather than an elective skill. The narrative is not just about employability but about shaping an identity: coding as the new piano, robotics as the new violin. These programmes are marketed as essential preparation for a future dominated by artificial intelligence and automation. Yet they are priced far beyond the reach of most households, meaning that only a narrow stratum of society is being groomed for this technologically saturated future. *The children of the affluent are not only being educated for tomorrow's jobs—they are being positioned to shape tomorrow's economy.*

Global disparities add another dimension. In the United States, elite families leverage platforms such as Khan Academy, Outschool, or Coursera to supplement schoolwork, often hiring tutors to personalise the experience. In China, the boom in edtech has been particularly stark; before recent government regulation, wealthy families were spending vast sums on online tutoring platforms to give their children a competitive edge in national examinations. Meanwhile, in parts of Africa, South Asia, or Latin America, where connectivity and devices remain uneven, digital enrichment opportunities are rare and sporadic. The children who might benefit most from personalised, flexible digital education are often the least likely to receive it, not for lack of ability but for lack of infrastructure and affordability.

The philosophical stakes are clear: technology, once heralded as a democratising force, has become a differentiator of privilege. It is not simply that the rich have more devices; it is that they have access to *better* devices, *better* platforms, and *better* integration of these tools into their learning lives. They also have parents with the time, resources, and digital fluency to curate educational pathways, filtering noise from value and enforcing disciplined use. *Digital literacy is no longer merely about knowing how to operate technology—it is about having the social scaffolding to extract its maximum potential.*

Critics argue that this dynamic risks entrenching inequality in subtle ways. In affluent households, technology is framed as a vehicle for creativity, exploration, and mastery. Children are encouraged to build apps, design digital art, or debate global issues in online forums. In under-resourced schools and families, technology is too often reduced to test-prep drills, standardised software, or supervised screen time intended to maintain order. This divergence reflects a broader structural problem: the same tool that expands horizons for one child narrows them for another. The disparity lies not in the technology itself but in the context in which it is deployed.

Case studies reinforce this reality. In Finland, often lauded for its egalitarian education system, disparities have begun to emerge as wealthier parents supplement free schooling with digital enrichment through private platforms. In India, middle- and upper-class families increasingly invest in edtech giants like BYJU'S, which market themselves as indispensable companions to traditional schooling, while lower-income households struggle with affordability and connectivity, leaving their children dependent on underfunded public schools. In the United Kingdom, coding camps and STEM-oriented holiday schools proliferate among wealthier families, while disadvantaged students often encounter technology in limited and remedial ways.

The cultural capital framework provides a useful lens here. Pierre Bourdieu argued that families transmit not only economic resources but also cultural habits, tastes, and competencies that position their children advantageously in society. In today's context, *technology fluency has become a form of cultural capital*—a socially inherited advantage that separates those who can navigate, create, and lead in digital spaces from those who can only consume passively. For elites, coding, digital collaboration, and algorithmic thinking are not just skills but part of a broader cultural identity that signals status and future leadership. For others, the digital sphere remains a tool for functional literacy at best.

One might imagine that democratising access to technology could mitigate these divides. Yet the evidence suggests otherwise. Laptops in every classroom or tablets for every student are insufficient without parallel investments in guidance, training, and enrichment. What wealthier families buy is not the device itself but the *ecosystem of support*—skilled tutors, curated platforms, dedicated time, and parental involvement. These elements transform technology from a crutch into a tool, from a superficial aid into a deeper form of empowerment.

The long-term implications are troubling. If the gap between elite and non-elite learners continues to widen, digital inequality will harden into social stratification. The elites of tomorrow will not only have higher incomes and stronger credentials but also fluency in the tools that govern economies, politics, and culture. They will be the designers of platforms, the curators of digital norms, the architects of algorithmic systems. Meanwhile, those excluded from this enrichment will find themselves perpetually adapting to structures designed by others, their role confined to users rather than shapers.

There are, of course, counter-arguments. Some contend that the scalability of digital platforms offers unprecedented opportunities for levelling the playing field. Open educational resources, free coding tutorials, and peer-to-peer learning communities can, in theory, empower motivated learners regardless of wealth. Stories abound of self-taught programmers in Lagos or Jakarta who leverage free online resources to build successful careers. Yet even these narratives often obscure the hidden scaffolding of success: stable internet, personal determination, supportive communities. These resources may be "free," but they are not equally accessible in practice. The exceptions prove the rule.

If there is a path forward, it lies in recognising that digital equality requires more than devices and broadband; it requires a rethinking of how enrichment is distributed. Schools must not only provide access to hardware but also design curricula that embed creative, exploratory, and critical uses of technology for all students, not just those who can afford private tutors. Public investment in coding academies, digital mentorship schemes, and subsidised online platforms could help narrow the gap. But as long as enrichment remains a private good purchased in a competitive marketplace, *the digital divide will increasingly mirror—and magnify—existing class divides.*

The emergence of new educational elites underscores a central paradox: technology has the potential to democratise learning, but in practice it often functions as a mechanism of exclusion. The promise of equal access has been co-opted by unequal contexts, where wealth transforms the same tools into vastly different outcomes. Unless addressed, the future of education risks becoming not a story of shared advancement but of stratified opportunity, where the most digitally fluent are not necessarily the most talented but the most privileged.

Chapter 6
Attention in the Age of Distraction

Few assets are more valuable to learning than attention, yet it is also the resource most under siege in today's digital environment. Students often believe they can divide it endlessly, convinced that they can complete an essay while toggling between text messages, playlists, and social media feeds. The mythology of multitasking has become so embedded in youth culture that sustained concentration now appears almost quaint, even inefficient. But neuroscience tells a very different story. Far from enhancing productivity, constant task-switching fractures cognitive processes, weakens memory consolidation, and erodes the quality of understanding. *Attention is not infinitely divisible—it is a finite currency, and the modern attention economy is built on exploiting it to exhaustion.*

The problem is not only what students choose to do with their devices but what those devices are designed to do to them. Smartphones and laptops do not simply sit passively on a desk awaiting instruction; they are engineered to interrupt, to capture, to seduce. Notifications are not accidental pings but carefully tuned behavioural triggers, drawing from the same psychological insights that keep gamblers fixed on slot machines. Each vibration carries the possibility of novelty, and each flash of red signals urgency, ensuring that even in the midst of study, the mind is lured away from the work at hand. The effect is cumulative: fragmented learning sessions stitched together with interruptions rarely add up to deep comprehension. *Students are not just distracted by their devices—they are being distracted on purpose.*

Consider the classroom itself. In affluent schools where students are given tablets or laptops for every lesson, it is not uncommon for teachers to glance out across the room and see half their pupils toggling silently between Google Docs and social media tabs. In less-resourced settings, where students rely on their personal smartphones for research, the situation is often worse: educational uses are constantly competing with the immediate gratification of messaging apps and entertainment platforms. Teachers attempt to redirect attention, but the struggle is uneven. The classroom is no longer just a space of teacher and student; it is an arena where commercial platforms and pedagogical aims are in direct competition.

The cognitive consequences are well documented. Studies reveal that task-switching carries a "switch cost," a measurable lag in mental performance every time attention shifts. What students often interpret as multitasking is in fact rapid serial switching, with each jump incurring a cognitive toll. Over time, this pattern fosters what psychologists call "shallow processing": students may remember fragments of information long enough to complete a task, but they fail to integrate those fragments into long-term understanding. The sense of productivity is illusory. They are busy but not learning, occupied but not transformed. *The more fragmented the learning environment, the weaker the intellectual gains.*

Yet it is important to resist framing this issue as merely a problem of student discipline. The platforms themselves bear responsibility. Social media companies and app developers devote immense resources to designing experiences that maximise engagement, often at the expense of sustained focus. Infinite scroll features, autoplay functions, and algorithmic feeds are not neutral—they are deliberate design choices optimised for retention. When students attempt to use these same devices for learning, they are effectively trying to study in an environment built to dismantle their concentration. Expecting adolescents to resist such mechanisms without support is less a matter of personal responsibility than of structural impossibility.

This tension has significant implications for education. On one hand, technology offers extraordinary opportunities: instant access to knowledge, interactive simulations, and global collaboration. On the other, it introduces vulnerabilities that reshape the very conditions of learning. For some students, especially those with strong parental or institutional guidance, technology becomes a powerful amplifier of curiosity and mastery. For others, particularly those without strong scaffolding, it becomes a constant source of distraction that hollows out learning from within. *Attention, once assumed to be a baseline in education, has become a new form of inequality—differentiating those who can control their focus from those whose focus is constantly stolen.*

The challenge is not simply to reduce distraction but to cultivate new habits of digital mindfulness. This means designing educational environments—both at home and in classrooms—that actively reinforce the value of sustained attention. Schools that have begun to experiment with device-free periods or structured digital protocols often find that students relearn the rhythm of focus, and with it the satisfaction of deep engagement. At home, parents who model intentional use of technology send a powerful signal: devices are tools, not tyrants. Over time, such practices cultivate resilience against the pull of constant notifications and help students experience learning not as a fragmented duty but as a concentrated act of discovery.

This chapter explores these dynamics in depth: how the myth of multitasking persists despite overwhelming evidence against it, how cognitive overload diminishes genuine learning, how platform design exploits human vulnerability, and how healthier digital habits might be cultivated. The stakes are not trivial. The ability to focus has become a marker of privilege, a skill increasingly scarce in an age of distraction yet increasingly valuable in a knowledge-driven world. *To attend fully is to learn deeply; to be perpetually distracted is to remain intellectually adrift. The difference may well determine who thrives and who falls behind in the digital age.*

The Myth of Multitasking

The conviction that young people can seamlessly juggle multiple tasks at once—switching between writing an essay, responding to messages, listening to music, and browsing social media—has become one of the most resilient illusions of the digital age. Students routinely defend the habit by pointing to their comfort with devices, as if fluency in toggling between tabs or apps translates into cognitive efficiency. Yet this confidence is at odds with what decades of neuroscience has demonstrated: *the human brain is not wired for true multitasking*. What appears as simultaneous attention is in fact rapid task-switching, and each switch carries a hidden cognitive cost that compounds over time. Far from expanding productivity, this pattern erodes memory, slows comprehension, and weakens the ability to engage in deep, sustained learning.

Understanding the persistence of this myth requires attention not only to cognitive science but also to the cultural environment in which students operate. Modern devices are designed to promote divided attention: multiple windows, layered notifications, and endless streams of content normalise a fractured experience of time and focus. In such a context, the act of concentrating on a single task begins to feel unnatural, even wasteful. For adolescents raised in this ecosystem, the expectation that learning should coexist with constant stimulation becomes almost second nature. The brain, however, does not evolve on the same schedule as technology. It retains limits shaped by biology, and those limits are unforgiving when ignored.

Research in cognitive psychology highlights a phenomenon known as "switch cost," the mental tax incurred whenever attention shifts from one task to another. Even when these shifts occur in fractions of a second, the residue of the previous activity lingers, impairing performance on the next. A student writing an essay while intermittently checking notifications is not performing two tasks in parallel but repeatedly interrupting one to attend to the other, with each interruption leaving traces of interference. The result is slower writing, more errors, and a thinner grasp of the material. When multiplied across hours of study, days of revision, or entire semesters of coursework, this effect produces a measurable deficit in learning outcomes. *What students interpret as productivity is often little more than cognitive self-sabotage disguised by activity.*

Consider also the impact on memory consolidation. Neuroscience shows that the transfer of information from short-term to long-term storage requires periods of undivided attention. Every time focus is disrupted, the process is interrupted, increasing the likelihood that material will be forgotten. This is why a student who studies while checking their phone may recall enough to perform acceptably on a short quiz but struggle to retain the knowledge weeks later. Deep learning—the kind that underpins problem-solving, creativity, and adaptability—demands sustained attention. Fragmented study sessions might feel efficient, but they produce knowledge that is brittle and fleeting.

Despite this, the narrative of the "digital multitasker" persists. Part of the explanation lies in psychology itself: multitasking creates a sense of busyness that can be mistaken for productivity. Students feel accomplished because they are constantly active, but activity is not synonymous with achievement. The dopamine rewards triggered by checking messages or scrolling through feeds reinforce the cycle, providing short bursts of satisfaction that mask the long-term cognitive cost. The allure is not unlike that of junk food:

immediately gratifying but nutritionally poor. Sustained attention, by contrast, is harder to maintain and less immediately rewarding, but it builds intellectual resilience in ways that fractured focus cannot.

Educational contexts often compound the problem. In classrooms where laptops are open, even diligent students are tempted to oscillate between tasks, rationalising that a few seconds spent glancing at unrelated material will not matter. Yet research consistently shows that even minor distractions degrade comprehension, and the presence of multitasking peers further diminishes learning by creating "second-hand distraction." A student sitting next to someone browsing social media will often find their own focus eroded, not by their own choice but by peripheral awareness. In this sense, the costs of multitasking extend beyond the individual to the collective environment of learning.

The cultural valorisation of multitasking also deserves scrutiny. In workplaces, students see adults praised for handling multiple demands at once, reinforcing the idea that cognitive juggling is a valuable skill. Popular culture portrays multitasking as a hallmark of competence, particularly in high-pressure fields. Yet the most effective professionals—surgeons, pilots, researchers—are trained to cultivate singular focus precisely because the stakes of distraction are so high. The difference is that these professions recognise attention as a scarce resource, whereas educational settings often treat it as abundant. *In reality, focus is not an optional luxury in learning; it is the foundation upon which all other skills rest.*

Some students do appear less vulnerable to the pitfalls of divided attention, which has fuelled the myth further. They claim to perform better with background music or to absorb information while messaging friends. Here it is important to distinguish between tasks that compete for the same cognitive resources and those that do not. Listening to instrumental music while reading may not demand the same linguistic processing systems, allowing some students to sustain comprehension. But attempting to draft an essay while responding to texts is a different matter: both activities draw on linguistic and executive function, ensuring interference. What feels like an exception is usually a misinterpretation of the type of task, not evidence of superhuman cognitive ability.

The myth of multitasking also obscures an important generational inequality. Students with access to environments that limit distractions—quiet study spaces, structured parental guidance, schools that enforce device management—develop an advantage in cultivating sustained attention. Those without such support are more likely to normalise fragmented learning as inevitable. Over time, the disparity becomes self-reinforcing: one group builds the cognitive endurance required for higher-order thinking, while the other struggles with surface-level engagement. In this sense, the myth is not just scientifically unfounded but socially damaging, because it justifies environments that make deep learning harder to achieve.

To counter this, educators and parents need to frame attention not as an archaic discipline but as a modern literacy. Just as students are taught to evaluate sources or construct arguments, they must also learn to manage the conditions of their own focus. This does not mean banning technology outright but recognising when and how it interferes with cognitive processes. Practical interventions—such as device-free study periods, structured note-taking, or guided digital use—can help re-establish attention as a skill to be cultivated rather than a default state to be taken for granted. Over time, such strategies can puncture the myth of multitasking by offering students direct experience of the difference between fractured and focused learning.

Ultimately, the belief in multitasking reveals a deeper cultural misunderstanding: the conflation of doing more with learning more. Students live in a world that equates busyness with value, and multitasking seems to promise efficiency in a culture that prizes speed. But the reality is harsher: the brain pays a steep price for every shift in attention, and the cumulative cost is profound. *To learn deeply is to focus deeply, and there is no shortcut through constant distraction.* If education is to prepare students for the complexity of tomorrow's world, dismantling the myth of multitasking is not a matter of preference but of necessity.

Cognitive Overload and Fragmented Learning

Few forces are as corrosive to genuine learning as the persistent drip of digital interruptions. Notifications, alerts, and constant task-switching not only compete for attention but also overwhelm the brain's capacity to process information. What makes this phenomenon particularly insidious is that it often masquerades as productivity: the rapid checking of messages, the quick response to an email, the toggling between lecture notes and search results. The activity feels industrious, yet beneath the surface the mind is fragmenting its focus, eroding comprehension, and quietly sabotaging long-term retention. *Cognitive overload is not simply a matter of being busy; it is a structural condition of modern learning environments in which the brain is asked to do more than it is designed to manage.*

At the core of this problem lies the brain's working memory—the limited mental workspace that temporarily holds and manipulates information. Cognitive science has long established that working memory is finite, often described as being able to hold around seven items at once, though in practice the number is usually lower when tasks are complex or unfamiliar. When students attempt to juggle multiple streams of input—say, a live lecture, incoming texts, and background social media—the working memory becomes saturated. Once that capacity is exceeded, new information either fails to register or displaces what was already there. This explains why students immersed in a swirl of notifications may leave study sessions with the unsettling sense of having "done a lot" but retained little of substance.

The design of digital platforms intensifies this vulnerability. Notifications are engineered to demand immediate attention, leveraging the brain's sensitivity to novelty and social cues. Each vibration or pop-up represents not merely a minor inconvenience but a redirection of cognitive resources. Returning to the original task requires re-establishing context, which consumes additional working memory and creates what psychologists term *attention residue*. The residue of the previous task lingers, muddying focus and reducing efficiency on the next. When such interruptions accumulate across an hour of study, the brain spends more time recalibrating than learning.

Real-world research bears this out. Experiments at Stanford and elsewhere have shown that so-called "heavy media multitaskers" perform worse on tests of memory, comprehension, and even the ability to filter irrelevant information. Their brains, conditioned by constant switching, struggle to ignore distractions even when instructed to do so. The very habit of frequent interruption reshapes attention itself, making it harder to sustain focus in environments that demand it. This creates a cruel paradox: students who lean most heavily on digital multitasking become less capable of concentrating when concentration is most required, such as during exams, professional training, or creative problem-solving.

Fragmented learning, however, is not simply a cognitive problem but a pedagogical one. Many educational systems inadvertently normalise it by integrating technology without addressing its psychological consequences. Online courses may encourage students to keep multiple tabs open, while schools that distribute devices often neglect to teach strategies for managing attention. Even well-meaning digital initiatives risk amplifying overload if they deliver a constant flow of notifications—updates, quizzes, reminders—that slice learning into micro-fragments. What is lost in this process is the depth of engagement that characterises true education: the immersion in a complex text, the sustained grappling with a difficult problem, the unbroken dialogue of a seminar. *Without depth, learning risks collapsing into a thin stream of disconnected facts rather than a durable structure of understanding.*

The effects of cognitive overload are not distributed evenly. Students with higher self-regulation skills or supportive home environments may learn to compartmentalise their focus, silencing notifications during study periods or creating physical separation between work and distraction. Others, particularly those in crowded households or under pressure to remain constantly available to family or peers, find themselves perpetually vulnerable to interruption. This inequality compounds over time: while one group accumulates the benefits of deep focus, the other habituates to shallow engagement. The divide is not merely technological but cognitive, shaping who develops the habits of mind most valued in higher education and professional life.

It is also worth noting the emotional dimension of overload. The relentless stream of information creates not only cognitive strain but also anxiety. Students often feel a pressure to respond instantly to digital cues, interpreting silence as negligence. This pressure keeps the brain in a state of heightened alert, further depleting working memory and undermining the calm concentration conducive to learning. In extreme cases, the cycle produces a state akin to burnout: exhaustion not from physical effort but from the relentless management of fragmented attention. In this sense, cognitive overload is as much about emotional sustainability as intellectual performance.

Some argue that students, having grown up in digital environments, have adapted to manage this constant flow. Yet the evidence suggests otherwise. Familiarity with technology does not erase biological constraints; the brain's architecture remains stubbornly resistant to demands for parallel processing. Adaptation may occur at the level of habit—students grow comfortable with interruptions—but comfort should not be mistaken for capacity. In fact, normalising distraction may reduce awareness of its costs, making students less likely to recognise the erosion of their comprehension and memory. *The adaptation is behavioural, not neurological, and it works against rather than with the demands of deep learning.*

Educational responses to this challenge are uneven. Some institutions have implemented "digital hygiene" practices—blocking notifications during classes, structuring online learning environments to minimise extraneous alerts, or teaching mindfulness-based strategies for attention management. Others remain wedded to the assumption that more technology necessarily means more progress, flooding students with digital platforms without accounting for the cumulative cognitive toll. The gap between these approaches underscores a crucial insight: technology itself is not the problem, but the uncritical way it is integrated into learning environments can tip the balance from enrichment to overload.

Ultimately, the struggle against cognitive overload requires reframing how we think about attention. Attention is not an inexhaustible commodity but a limited resource, more akin to physical stamina than to a switch that can be turned on and off at will. Every notification, every task-switch, every moment of fragmented focus depletes that resource. To treat attention with care is not to resist technology but to recognise its demands and to design learning environments that protect the brain's limited capacity for processing. In doing so, educators can preserve what makes learning transformative: the ability not just to consume information but to integrate, reflect, and create meaning from it.

Cognitive overload and fragmented learning are not peripheral challenges; they go to the heart of what education aims to achieve. If the goal is comprehension, retention, and the cultivation of deep intellectual skills, then the constant slicing of attention is antithetical to progress. The future of learning depends not on students' ability to manage ever more streams of input, but on society's willingness to acknowledge the limits of the mind and to create conditions where attention can once again serve as the foundation of knowledge.

Platform Design and Student Vulnerability

The digital platforms that dominate modern life are rarely designed with learning in mind. Their architecture is tuned to maximise engagement, measured in minutes on screen, clicks, and advertising revenue rather than comprehension, reflection, or intellectual growth. What looks like a harmless notification system, an endless scroll, or a recommendation carousel is in fact the product of deliberate psychological engineering. *Students today are not simply passive users of technology; they are subjects of attention economies whose incentives are often fundamentally misaligned with the aims of education.*

At the heart of these designs lies the principle of variable rewards, a behavioural mechanism famously observed in experiments with animals pressing levers for unpredictable treats. Social media feeds and video platforms employ the same logic: one swipe may deliver something amusing, another something informative, the next something utterly trivial, but the uncertainty keeps the user engaged. For students, this unpredictability collides with study habits. The attempt to revise a lesson or write an essay is repeatedly punctured by the lure of refreshing a feed or checking for likes, not because the student lacks discipline but because the platform is engineered to override self-control. *The vulnerability here is structural, not moral; it reflects design priorities that monetise distraction rather than knowledge.*

The consequences for education are profound. A platform like YouTube may contain lectures of extraordinary quality, yet its interface steers learners towards recommended content designed to hold attention, not deepen understanding. A student searching for a physics explanation can be nudged towards entertainment clips within minutes, pulled away not by conscious choice but by the gravitational pull of an algorithm that measures success by watch time. Similarly, messaging apps blur boundaries between study and social life, fostering environments where concentration is constantly at risk of fracture. What emerges is a paradox: the very tools that could democratise access to knowledge often undermine the conditions needed to internalise it.

Research into platform design confirms how deeply these mechanisms shape behaviour. Eye-tracking studies reveal that bright badges, alerts, and red icons draw attention away from the central task, exploiting the brain's sensitivity to visual salience. Neurological evidence shows that each small interruption activates the brain's reward pathways, producing a brief surge of dopamine that reinforces the habit of checking. Over time, this neurological conditioning reshapes attentional habits themselves, training students to expect and even crave disruption. In educational contexts, this leads to what psychologists describe as *attentional drift*: the difficulty of sustaining focus on non-stimulating but essential tasks, such as deep reading or problem-solving.

The problem is compounded by the fact that students are not equal in their capacity to resist these designs. Those with greater parental guidance, access to quiet study environments, or explicit training in digital literacy may learn to set boundaries—silencing notifications, using focus apps, or structuring work sessions to minimise distraction. Others, particularly in environments where technology is both entertainment and education, are left exposed to the full weight of attention-capturing design. The disparity becomes a hidden amplifier of inequality: while one group leverages technology as a genuine learning tool, another finds its cognitive resources siphoned away by the very platforms that promise empowerment.

Some educators argue that the problem lies not in the platforms themselves but in how students use them. They point to the immense value of open educational resources, online tutorials, and collaborative tools that exist alongside the distractions. Yet this argument risks underestimating the asymmetry between intention and design. A student may log in with the best of intentions, but the platform's architecture is not neutral; it actively works to redirect attention. To place responsibility solely on the student is to ignore the deliberate strategies of the digital attention economy. *Expecting young learners to resist billion-dollar designs optimised to exploit psychological weaknesses is neither realistic nor fair.*

The educational consequences extend beyond momentary distraction. When learning becomes interspersed with fragmented attention, comprehension suffers, and so does the ability to build coherent knowledge structures. Students habituated to constant platform switching often struggle with sustained analytical tasks, such as writing extended essays or engaging in deep discussions. More subtly, they may lose confidence in their capacity for focus itself, internalising the belief that prolonged concentration is unattainable. This erosion of self-belief is as damaging as the immediate cognitive costs, undermining resilience in academic and professional pursuits.

There are, however, emerging examples of alternative design. Some educational platforms deliberately structure interfaces to reduce cognitive overload, avoiding unnecessary alerts and privileging linear progression over endless recommendation loops. Mindfulness-inspired apps encourage learners to pause, reflect, and engage deeply with content rather than skim. Even mainstream technology companies, under pressure from researchers and regulators, have introduced features such as "focus modes" or daily time limits. Yet these remain optional layers atop a system still fundamentally organised around engagement metrics. The broader challenge is to shift the cultural and economic logic of platforms from maximising clicks to cultivating comprehension.

For educators, awareness of platform design has become an essential part of pedagogy. Teaching digital literacy now requires more than showing students how to search or evaluate sources; it involves unpacking the mechanics of attention capture and giving learners tools to navigate them. This may mean explicitly discussing the business models of platforms, helping students recognise the nudges built into interfaces, or creating classroom practices that model deep, uninterrupted work. In some contexts, it involves rethinking the integration of technology altogether—deciding when the cognitive costs outweigh the potential benefits. *The task is not to reject digital tools wholesale but to reassert control over how they are used, ensuring that educational priorities rather than commercial incentives dictate design choices.*

The vulnerability of students to platform design highlights a deeper philosophical question: what does it mean to be free in a digital world? If autonomy rests on the ability to direct one's attention, then platforms that systematically hijack that attention undermine not only learning but also agency itself. Education, at its best, is a process of cultivating independence of thought, yet when the very tools of learning compromise attention, they risk narrowing rather than expanding intellectual horizons. This tension demands critical engagement not just from educators but from policymakers, technologists, and students themselves.

Ultimately, the issue is not that students are weak-willed or careless but that they are placed in environments structured to erode focus. Until design incentives shift, education must grapple with the reality that the platforms shaping young people's cognitive habits are not neutral. Recognising this misalignment is the first step towards reclaiming technology as a tool for learning rather than a trap for attention. Only then can students begin to engage with digital tools on their own terms, harnessing their potential for knowledge rather than being consumed by their architecture of distraction.

Toward Digital Mindfulness

The greatest challenge of digital learning is not access to devices or the abundance of online resources, but the erosion of attention that occurs when those devices dominate daily life. The very tools that promise empowerment often sow habits of distraction, leaving both students and teachers trapped in cycles of fractured focus. What is needed is not a rejection of technology but the cultivation of a new discipline: *digital mindfulness*, the deliberate shaping of habits that enable technology to serve education rather than undermine it.

Mindfulness in this context does not mean meditation apps or wellness slogans; it means conscious structuring of how, when, and why digital tools are used. At its core, digital mindfulness is about reclaiming agency in environments designed to erode it. A notification is not merely a sound but a demand on attention; an infinite scroll is not just a design choice but a cognitive trap. When students learn to see these mechanisms clearly, they can begin to resist them. This is not simply a personal virtue but a social necessity, for without conscious strategies, the architecture of the digital world will shape behaviour by default.

One model comes from classrooms that have reimagined the relationship between devices and learning time. Some schools have implemented "attention zoning," where devices are used intensively for short, purposeful bursts followed by structured offline reflection. Rather than banning technology altogether—a strategy that often fails in the long term—teachers guide students in alternating between digital engagement and analogue consolidation. A lesson might involve a twenty-minute exploration of an online archive, followed by handwritten notes or group discussion without screens. This rhythm not only protects attention but teaches students that technology is a tool to be used deliberately, not a constant background presence.

At home, families adopting similar strategies find that simple rules yield disproportionate benefits. Shared charging stations keep devices out of bedrooms at night, reinforcing sleep hygiene and reducing late-night scrolling. Designated "tech-free meals" preserve conversational space, modelling to young people that not all interactions must be mediated by screens. Such rules may appear modest, but they restore boundaries in an environment where none exist by default. *The insight is that healthier digital habits rarely emerge spontaneously; they require structures that make attentional discipline visible and shared.*

The psychological benefits of digital mindfulness are reinforced by neuroscientific evidence. Studies show that constant task-switching impairs the brain's ability to transfer information from short-term to long-term memory, while periods of sustained, undistracted focus enhance comprehension. When classrooms and households adopt practices that encourage immersion in single tasks, they are not merely cultivating etiquette—they are rewiring neural pathways that support deep learning. The cultivation of these habits is especially critical for younger learners whose attentional systems are still developing, and who are therefore more vulnerable to long-term shaping by digital environments.

Critics of mindfulness-oriented approaches sometimes dismiss them as nostalgic or unrealistic, arguing that modern life requires constant connectivity and that students must adapt rather than resist. Yet this framing misinterprets adaptation. The goal is not to withdraw from digital spaces but to *use them with awareness*. A student who learns to silence notifications during study is not retreating from the modern world but mastering it. The capacity to control one's attention is increasingly a form of capital, distinguishing those who thrive in digital environments from those who are consumed by them.

In some contexts, technology itself can be harnessed to foster mindfulness. Tools that block distracting sites during study sessions, track screen time, or provide "focus modes" show how design can be reoriented to support rather than undermine attention. Yet these tools are only effective when paired with intentional practices and critical understanding. Otherwise, they risk becoming yet another layer of digital dependency. The most effective models integrate technology as a conscious partner in habit formation rather than as an external enforcer. For example, students who use time-tracking apps alongside reflective journaling learn not only how much time they spend online but *why* they drift into certain patterns, transforming data into insight.

Cultural differences also shape the practice of digital mindfulness. In some East Asian schools, collective rituals—such as placing phones in lockers at the start of the day—embed attentional discipline into shared routines. In contrast, Western classrooms often emphasise individual choice, leaving responsibility with students. Both approaches reveal tensions between autonomy and structure. A balanced model may combine the two, giving students increasing freedom as they demonstrate the capacity to regulate their own use. What matters is that attentional discipline is taught and reinforced, not left to chance.

The practice of digital mindfulness also invites broader philosophical reflection on the meaning of education. If the purpose of schooling is not only to transmit knowledge but to form habits of thought, then the way students engage with digital tools becomes central to pedagogy. Teachers who prioritise mindfulness are not simply managing distractions; they are teaching a deeper lesson about what it means to think clearly in a noisy world. This lesson extends beyond the classroom into every domain of life, preparing students not just for exams but for participation in civic and professional spaces where attention is constantly contested.

Parents, too, play a decisive role. Research shows that children emulate parental digital habits far more than they follow rules. A parent who urges a child to focus while constantly checking emails themselves communicates a double standard. Families that practise collective mindfulness—limiting devices during shared time, modelling attentive listening, and discussing digital choices openly—create cultures where healthier habits feel natural rather than imposed. *In this sense, digital mindfulness is not a programme to be delivered but a culture to be lived.*

None of this is simple. The attention economy is powerful precisely because it operates invisibly, exploiting cognitive vulnerabilities at scale. Cultivating digital mindfulness requires constant reinforcement, shared commitment, and institutional support. Schools cannot succeed if homes undermine their efforts, and parents cannot succeed if schools normalise unreflective device use. Nor can individuals be expected to shoulder the burden without broader structural change. The challenge, then, is to align families, educators, and policymakers around practices that place human attention—arguably the scarcest resource of the digital age—at the centre of educational design.

The promise of digital technology in education is immense, but it will only be realised if learners are equipped to manage its risks. Digital mindfulness offers not a retreat from technology but a blueprint for living well within it. By cultivating deliberate habits in classrooms and homes, by designing environments that privilege focus over distraction, and by teaching students to see through the mechanisms that compete for their attention, we can reclaim technology as a servant of learning rather than its master. The task is urgent, but it is also hopeful: for while platforms are powerful, the capacity to use them wisely remains within our grasp.

Chapter 7
The Parent Gap

The role of parents in shaping children's digital lives is often treated as peripheral, a matter of supervision or rule-setting. Yet the reality is far more complex and consequential. In a world where digital technologies mediate learning, communication, and even play, parents are no longer just guardians of safety; they are de facto educators. Their influence determines not simply how much time a child spends online, but what they take from it, how they discern information, and whether technology becomes a tool of growth or a source of dependency. The stakes are high, for *parental engagement in digital literacy is fast becoming one of the most significant predictors of long-term educational outcomes.*

The distinction between guidance and policing sits at the heart of this tension. Many households rely on limits and prohibitions—time caps on screen use, blocked apps, Wi-Fi curfews—as their primary form of intervention. These measures provide structure, but they do little to cultivate discernment. A child may spend fewer hours on a device, but without coaching they may still fall prey to misinformation, manipulation, or shallow consumption. True guidance requires active involvement: sitting alongside children, discussing what they see online, contextualising digital interactions, and modelling balanced use. The difference is profound: policing manages exposure, while guidance develops capacity. One is reactive, the other developmental.

Socioeconomic factors intensify this divide. Parents with higher levels of education and digital fluency are often able to frame technology as opportunity—using it to expand vocabulary, explore interests, or connect children to new learning communities. In contrast, parents with limited digital skills or time frequently rely on devices as stand-ins for supervision. This is not a matter of carelessness but of constrained resources. A single parent working long hours may depend on tablets to occupy children after school; a family without reliable broadband may default to whatever content loads most easily. *In practice, the quality of digital engagement a child receives is as much about a household's circumstances as it is about parental intent.*

The phenomenon of outsourcing learning to devices illustrates this dynamic starkly. Tablets and educational apps are marketed as tutors, promising personalised instruction at scale. In wealthier households, such tools are often supplemented by live guidance, with parents or hired tutors helping children navigate, interpret, and apply what they encounter. In under-resourced homes, however, devices frequently operate in isolation, functioning as electronic babysitters. The result is that two children may spend equal time on "educational technology" but emerge with vastly different outcomes. One learns to integrate digital knowledge into a broader intellectual framework, while the other becomes adept at navigating interfaces but remains shallow in comprehension.

Bridging the intergenerational divide is therefore essential. Many parents grew up in an analogue world and approach technology with either suspicion or resignation. Their children, by contrast, inhabit digital environments fluently yet often without critical awareness. The danger is that this asymmetry fosters distance rather than dialogue. When parents default to prohibition because they cannot understand platforms themselves, children learn to conceal usage rather than share it. When parents assume that young people are "digital natives" who require no guidance, they abdicate responsibility entirely. The challenge is to create a culture of co-learning: parents admitting what they do not know, exploring platforms together, and modelling curiosity in the face of new tools. Such collaboration not only reduces the gap in digital skills but fosters trust, making children more likely to seek advice rather than hide mistakes.

This intergenerational co-learning carries broader social significance. It reframes technology not as a wedge that separates generations but as a shared frontier. Parents who embrace this approach become more than regulators; they become mentors. Their children, in turn, come to see digital life not as a secret domain beyond adult understanding but as part of a collective conversation about values, risks, and opportunities. In societies already fractured by inequalities of income and education, such practices can mitigate the reproduction of disadvantage. They ensure that digital fluency is not confined to elites who can afford tutors and academies but is cultivated within families of all kinds.

The parent gap is thus not merely about rules or literacy, but about the formation of digital citizenship itself. To close it requires more than software controls or policy directives. It demands recognition that parents are central actors in the digital education of their children, whether or not they see themselves as such. By shifting from policing to guidance, by addressing socioeconomic constraints, and by embracing intergenerational co-learning, families can transform technology from a source of division into a space of shared growth. The question is not whether parents will shape their children's digital lives, but *how*—through absent control or through active, engaged, and reflective guidance.

Guidance vs. Policing

Parents across the world confront a paradox when raising children in the digital age: technology is both indispensable and potentially corrosive. For many, the instinctive response has been control—limiting screen time, setting curfews on devices, blocking apps, or monitoring activity through parental control software. These strategies, while comforting in their clarity, fail to address the more subtle challenge: helping children develop the discernment required to navigate a digital world that cannot simply be switched off. *The deeper question is not how long children spend online, but how they spend that time and what habits of mind they cultivate in the process.*

The distinction between policing and guidance is often blurred in practice, yet the difference is profound. Policing is rooted in external control: restrictions imposed from above, usually with the assumption that children are unable to regulate themselves. It can prevent harm in the short term, particularly for younger children, but it rarely fosters resilience or self-management. Guidance, by contrast, is participatory. It acknowledges that children must eventually learn to govern their own digital lives, and it involves coaching them in the skills of evaluation, critical inquiry, and responsible participation. A parent who simply locks down a phone at 8 p.m. curtails use; a parent who discusses why endless scrolling diminishes concentration teaches a principle that travels with the child long after restrictions fall away.

Research on adolescent psychology underscores this tension. Studies show that authoritarian control—strict limits without explanation—often breeds secrecy rather than compliance. Children subject to such rules learn to hide their online activity, or they become skilled at circumventing controls, undermining the very protection those rules are meant to provide. Conversely, when parents adopt what psychologists term an *authoritative style*—firm boundaries combined with reasoning, dialogue, and involvement—children tend to develop healthier digital habits, greater trust in their caregivers, and better long-term outcomes. The distinction reflects a broader truth: *monitoring may control behaviour, but only engagement shapes values.*

The risks of relying solely on policing become evident when we consider how digital environments evolve. Algorithms, interfaces, and online cultures shift constantly; new apps can emerge and dominate within months. Rules designed for one platform often collapse under the weight of another. A household may block TikTok, only to discover that YouTube Shorts or Instagram Reels provide identical temptations. Guidance, by contrast, is portable. A conversation about the psychology of infinite scroll remains relevant across platforms. An explanation of why misinformation spreads quickly on social media arms a child to approach both current and future platforms with scepticism. Restriction locks the door; guidance equips the traveller.

Consider the example of online gaming, a common flashpoint in families. A policing approach might set a fixed two-hour limit and enforce it with timers. This prevents overuse but may do little to address the underlying dynamics of the game itself: the social pressures of multiplayer play, the mechanics of in-game rewards, or the risks of online harassment. A guidance approach would involve sitting with the child, asking questions about the nature of the game, and exploring together the balance between enjoyment and overindulgence. Such involvement not only informs the parent but validates the child's experience, showing that their digital world is not invisible or irrelevant to the adult sphere.

Socioeconomic factors complicate this picture further. Families with limited resources may lean more heavily on policing simply because guidance requires time, energy, and digital literacy that not all parents possess. For a working parent juggling multiple jobs, installing time limits may feel like the only viable form of intervention. Yet children in these contexts are often the very ones who most need active coaching, since their access to digital role models is otherwise limited. This creates a new dimension of inequality: affluent households may cultivate digital discernment through dialogue, while less resourced families rely on blunt restrictions, leaving children less prepared to navigate the complexity of online life independently.

One philosophical objection sometimes raised is that children, being "digital natives," do not require guidance at all. Because they appear adept at navigating devices and apps, the assumption is that they understand them deeply. Yet fluency in interface is not the same as literacy in content. A child can swipe, search, and post without grasping the economic incentives behind the platforms, the mechanics of data collection, or the ways in which attention is commodified. This is why guidance is not about teaching children *how* to use technology—they already know—but about teaching them *how to think about their use of technology.* Without that reflective layer, even skilled digital users risk becoming passive consumers of environments designed to manipulate their choices.

Critics of guidance sometimes argue that it is too idealistic, that children will not listen or that dialogue cannot compete with the pull of screens. Yet evidence suggests otherwise. When children feel that their digital worlds are understood and respected, they are more likely to invite parental involvement. Moreover, guidance does not require constant oversight. It can be embedded in small, consistent practices: asking a child about the source of an online video, sharing an article that illustrates bias in a news feed, or reflecting aloud on one's own moments of digital distraction. Such gestures accumulate, signalling to children that digital life is not a private realm divorced from adult wisdom, but part of the shared fabric of family life.

The shift from policing to guidance also reframes what it means to prepare children for adulthood. Restrictions are temporary; eventually, young people will leave households and enter environments where no one limits their notifications or filters their feeds. If their only preparation has been policing, they may be unprepared to manage autonomy.

Guidance, by contrast, anticipates that moment. It teaches principles that endure: the value of focus, the recognition of manipulation, the practice of pausing before sharing content. These are the skills of digital citizenship, not merely digital survival.

The debate between guidance and policing, then, is not simply about parenting style but about educational philosophy. Do we want to raise children who comply with external controls, or individuals who can reason, discern, and act with agency in digital spaces? The former may yield short-term peace at home, but the latter is indispensable in a world where technology pervades every sphere of work, politics, and culture. *The true task of parents is not to shield children from the digital world but to prepare them to move through it wisely.*

Guidance is demanding. It requires knowledge, humility, and time. But it is also transformative. It positions parents not as wardens of digital life but as partners in its exploration. By choosing guidance over policing, families do more than regulate devices; they shape habits of mind that will determine whether the next generation inhabits technology passively or masters it critically. The difference, though subtle in the day-to-day, will echo across lifetimes.

Socioeconomic Factors in Parental Involvement

When it comes to children's digital learning, the greatest differentiator is often not access to devices or internet connections, but the role parents play in shaping how technology is used. Here, socioeconomic factors reveal their profound weight. The digital home is not a neutral space; it is mediated by parents' knowledge, time, confidence, and capacity to intervene. *A tablet may look the same in every household, but what it represents—a portal to enrichment or a distraction machine—depends largely on the literacy and involvement of the adults who set its context.*

Parental tech literacy operates as an invisible form of capital, one that divides children into those who learn to use technology as a ladder and those who become trapped in its loops. Parents with higher levels of education or professional backgrounds in digital environments tend to model practices of discerning search, critical evaluation, and productive use. They are more likely to know about privacy settings, spot misleading information, or encourage their children to create rather than simply consume content. By contrast, parents with less digital familiarity may feel intimidated or excluded, leading to hands-off approaches where children are left to self-navigate environments designed by powerful corporations to capture attention rather than cultivate skills. *The irony is stark: children of parents who need the most support in navigating digital complexity often receive the least guidance.*

Time compounds this inequality. Even parents who are digitally literate may lack the hours to engage meaningfully with their children's online worlds. A professional who works multiple shifts or juggles precarious employment cannot sit beside a child to explore the nuances of online safety or guide them through an educational platform. In such homes, technology often becomes a stand-in for parental presence—a babysitter, a distraction, or, in some cases, an unregulated tutor. Meanwhile, in households where time is more abundant, parents may accompany their children online, curating experiences, checking comprehension, and encouraging reflection. The difference is not simply one of screen-time limits, but of whether screen time becomes passive or purposeful.

Case studies across the globe reinforce this dynamic. In parts of Scandinavia, where parents are generally digitally fluent and have stronger work-life balance policies, children often receive active digital mentoring. Parents may discuss with their children how algorithms shape what they see or help them differentiate credible sources from spurious ones. Compare this with low-income communities in the United

States or rural areas of the Global South, where parents frequently express frustration at their inability to keep up with platforms their children master with ease. Here, children are more exposed to risks such as cyberbullying, misinformation, and unproductive bingeing, not because parents do not care, but because they lack the literacy or time to provide effective scaffolding.

The disparities extend to expectations as well. In middle- and upper-income households, parents increasingly treat digital engagement as something to be optimised. They enrol children in coding academies, encourage project-based use of technology, and frame digital skills as career investments. Devices in such homes become tools of advancement. For families under financial or social strain, however, digital use is more often tolerated than cultivated. If a child is quiet with a smartphone, that may be a relief rather than a cause for concern. *The same technology that is a springboard for some is a pacifier for others, not by design but by circumstance.*

The intergenerational dimension also deserves attention. Many parents in disadvantaged contexts grew up with little or no digital exposure themselves, creating a knowledge gap between them and their children. This generational inversion—where children are more competent than parents—disrupts traditional hierarchies of authority. A child who navigates platforms fluidly may dismiss parental input, while a parent who feels outpaced may retreat from engagement altogether. Wealthier households are better positioned to bridge this divide, not only because parents are more digitally adept, but also because they can outsource support: hiring tutors, investing in structured programmes, or leveraging extended networks of digitally literate relatives and peers.

Socioeconomic inequalities also appear in how parents conceptualise digital risks. In affluent families, concerns often focus on subtler issues—privacy, mental health, the erosion of concentration. In lower-income households, immediate anxieties dominate: exposure to harmful content, online predators, or simply the challenge of keeping children indoors in safe environments. The capacity to think beyond crisis management towards digital enrichment requires stability that not all families enjoy. Thus, while affluent parents prepare their children to be discerning creators in a knowledge economy, less resourced families may be forced into a defensive posture, focusing on harm prevention at the expense of long-term cultivation.

One might argue that schools should fill this gap, offering digital literacy training to level the playing field. Yet even where schools attempt this, the role of parents remains decisive. A child who receives reinforcement at home—where parents ask critical questions, encourage balanced habits, and participate in digital activities—consolidates skills far more effectively than a child who only encounters them in the classroom. As Pierre Bourdieu's concept of cultural capital reminds us, advantages are not merely about what schools teach but about the home environments in which learning is normalised and extended. Digital capital, like cultural capital, is inherited unequally, shaping children's capacity to thrive in digital ecosystems long before they reach professional life.

Philosophically, this raises a difficult question: should digital competence be considered a private family responsibility or a societal one? If we accept that digital literacy is as essential as reading or numeracy, then the stark disparities created by socioeconomic differences cannot be left to parental chance. Yet interventions are challenging. Parental digital training programmes often fail to attract those who most need them, either because of stigma, lack of time, or sheer exhaustion. Public policies can distribute devices, but they cannot distribute parental confidence, patience, or the subtle art of modelling digital wisdom.

There is, however, scope for reframing. Parents need not become technical experts to provide guidance; what matters is their willingness to engage. Asking children about what they are doing online, sharing curiosity, and reflecting together on experiences are practices within reach of most households. Programmes that build bridges between schools and parents—such as digital homework that encourages parent-child collaboration—can mitigate disparities by embedding shared learning moments. Similarly, workplaces that respect family time indirectly contribute to better digital mentoring, as parents with more balanced schedules are freer to be involved.

The socioeconomic factors shaping parental involvement are not just background conditions; they are active forces that structure the digital futures of children. The interplay of tech literacy, time, and cultural expectations determines whether devices serve as engines of growth or placeholders for absent guidance. The challenge is not merely one of equity in access to hardware, but of equity in access to human capital—the conversations, the coaching, and the confidence that transform technology from an indifferent tool into a formative force.

Ultimately, the story of children's digital lives is also the story of their parents' circumstances. Where parents possess the resources to guide, children learn to discern. Where parents are stretched too thin or excluded by knowledge gaps, children must improvise their own rules, often in environments stacked against them. *The digital divide is not only technological; it is deeply human, rooted in the uneven capacity of families to provide the guidance without which access becomes shallow and opportunity unequal.*

When Parents Outsource Learning to Devices

The device slipped into a child's hands often carries a double meaning. On one level it is a lifeline for parents under pressure: a tool that buys silence, occupies restless minds, and offers a momentary reprieve in households where time is scarce and demands are relentless. On another level it is an invisible educator, shaping habits, values, and modes of thinking in ways that parents neither monitor nor fully comprehend. *To outsource learning to devices is not a neutral act of convenience but a structural shift in how authority, knowledge, and responsibility are distributed in a child's life.*

The phenomenon has grown in parallel with economic and cultural pressures. Parents in many parts of the world now work longer hours, often without the support of extended family or affordable childcare. In this context, the phone or tablet is not merely entertainment but a form of delegation: handing over the role of supervision to algorithms and digital interfaces. Unlike the television of past decades, which offered limited and largely linear programming, today's devices are interactive, personalised, and designed to maximise engagement. This makes them more potent as teachers—yet their curriculum is not one of critical thought or structured knowledge, but of click patterns and attention capture.

The educational consequences of this outsourcing are uneven. On the one hand, there are cases where devices provide genuine enrichment. Children who access high-quality literacy apps, language learning platforms, or creative tools may benefit from expanded horizons that their parents, however well-meaning, could not provide. For migrant families, translation tools allow children to bridge linguistic divides; for rural households, online videos may expose learners to concepts absent in local schools. In these scenarios, devices appear as democratising forces, narrowing gaps in exposure. But these are the exceptions, requiring either intentional curation by parents or sheer luck in what children stumble upon. For the majority, the absence of active parental mediation means that devices default to their most commercially profitable role: vehicles of distraction.

Research in developmental psychology highlights the risks of leaving devices as surrogate instructors. Young children learn best through reciprocal interaction—back-and-forth dialogue, questioning, and social modelling. An app or video can simulate elements of this exchange but cannot replicate the nuance of parental feedback, the adjustment of explanations to a child's specific misunderstanding, or the relational warmth that encourages persistence. *When devices replace parents as teachers, what disappears is not only content but context: the subtle scaffolding that turns information into understanding.*

Consider the widespread practice of using YouTube to "teach" toddlers letters, numbers, or songs. While some children indeed pick up vocabulary or tunes, studies reveal that retention and transfer are weaker compared to learning through parental engagement. A child who repeats "A is for apple" after a video may not grasp the concept of letters as symbolic representations; a parent, sensing confusion, would adjust the explanation or offer tangible examples. Outsourced learning can create a veneer of competence that masks shallow comprehension.

The social consequences are equally pronounced. Parents who rely heavily on devices to occupy their children often do so at critical moments of social learning: meal times, car journeys, waiting rooms. These are precisely the spaces where children historically absorbed norms of conversation, patience, and observation. A tablet introduced as a pacifier interrupts these micro-moments of informal education, leaving children less practised in social cues and interpersonal negotiation. Teachers often note the effects in classrooms: students who struggle to sustain dialogue, wait their turn, or engage in sustained problem-solving because they are accustomed to rapid, stimulus-driven interaction.

Cultural expectations shape how this outsourcing is perceived. In affluent contexts, parents may justify device use by pointing to "educational" branding: the coding app, the maths game, the curated video channel. Yet even in these households, the line between learning and distraction is porous. What begins as practice in arithmetic can, within minutes, slide into hours of unrelated browsing, thanks to recommendation algorithms. In lower-income households, devices are more likely to be employed simply as digital babysitters, with little pretence of education. In both cases, however, the effect is a displacement of parental presence by a screen designed less to teach than to monetise attention.

Philosophically, the outsourcing of learning to devices raises questions about authority. Traditionally, parents mediated a child's relationship to knowledge—choosing books, filtering influences, and embedding values through shared practice. Now, corporations and platforms assume much of that role, subtly defining what content is available, how it is sequenced, and what values are implied. Parents who outsource are not just delegating time but surrendering a degree of cultural transmission. This becomes more troubling when one recognises that platforms are optimised for engagement rather than education. The lessons a child learns—instant gratification, endless choice, the erosion of patience—are rarely those a parent would consciously endorse.

Counterarguments exist. Some scholars suggest that digital devices foster self-directed learning, empowering children to explore interests without constant adult oversight. Indeed, there are examples of children teaching themselves coding, musical skills, or scientific concepts through online communities, often surpassing what their parents could have offered. But such outcomes typically depend on an underlying framework of parental encouragement and oversight, even if subtle. The paradox is that self-directed learning often thrives when parents are indirectly engaged—providing guardrails, encouragement, or contextual grounding. Absent this, self-direction can devolve into aimless browsing, with minimal cognitive growth.

The reliance on devices as substitutes also has unintended consequences for family dynamics. Parents who lean heavily on screens may feel guilt, sensing that their children are being short-changed of attention. Children, for their part, may experience confusion: they perceive the device as an authority but also as entertainment, blurring the line between serious learning and play. Over time, this can foster habits of superficial engagement, where "learning" is equated with watching videos rather than grappling with concepts. In adolescence, the stakes rise: devices become avenues for social validation, advertising, and ideology, all consumed without parental mediation. *What begins as a pragmatic compromise in early childhood can mature into a deeply ingrained habit of unfiltered digital dependence.*

Global comparisons reveal further nuance. In some parts of East Asia, where parental involvement in education is culturally intense, devices are often seen as extensions of tutoring regimes rather than as replacements for parental attention. Parents guide their use towards specific educational outcomes. In contrast, in parts of the Global South where resources and time are scarcer, devices become default caretakers, with little capacity for oversight. The outcomes, unsurprisingly, diverge. One context harnesses devices to amplify parental involvement, the other to substitute for it.

What is most striking is not that parents outsource, but the degree to which this outsourcing is normalised. Few public conversations address it directly, yet it is shaping an entire generation's relationship with knowledge and authority. The practice reflects broader societal values: convenience over patience, efficiency over presence, delegation over dialogue. If left unchecked, it risks creating a generation fluent in the mechanics of digital consumption but underdeveloped in the deeper skills of interpretation, persistence, and critical thought.

To address this, one need not demonise technology but rather reframe parental roles. Outsourcing can be softened into co-sourcing: where devices provide supplementary material, but parents remain the interpreters and moderators. Instead of handing over the tablet unconditionally, parents might sit with their child, ask questions about what they watch, or set tasks that require creative output. Even in time-pressed households, moments of shared reflection—"What did you learn?" or "Why do you think the video said that?"—can transform passive consumption into active engagement.

The reliance on devices as teachers is not inherently damaging, but unexamined reliance is. Without intentional mediation, children risk learning from systems designed for profit rather than growth. Parents who outsource entirely may discover too late that their children have mastered distraction more thoroughly than discernment. *The challenge is not whether devices can teach, but whether we as a society are content to let them teach alone.*

Bridging the Intergenerational Divide

The paradox of the digital age is that children often appear more adept with technology than the very parents responsible for guiding them. A child may instinctively swipe through an app, configure a new device, or navigate an unfamiliar platform with the ease of intuition, while their parent struggles with basic settings or online safety controls. This inversion of authority unsettles traditional family dynamics and raises pressing questions: how can parents provide meaningful guidance when their children seem to know more than they do? And what are the risks of leaving this gap unaddressed? *The answer lies not in restoring a hierarchy that no longer exists, but in reimagining learning as a collaborative process where both generations share responsibility for digital fluency.*

The digital divide between generations is not simply technical; it is also cultural and epistemic. Parents who grew up in analogue environments tend to view technology as a tool—something external, purposeful, and bounded. Children, by contrast, experience it as a habitat: an ever-present layer of reality that mediates communication, play, and even identity formation. This difference in perception shapes behaviours. A parent might treat screen time as a discrete activity to be regulated, while a child regards it as an integral part of social life. Bridging the divide, therefore, requires more than teaching parents the mechanics of devices. It demands a shift in mindset, where both sides learn to appreciate the other's perspective, blending technical knowledge with cultural interpretation.

One powerful starting point is to reframe digital skills as family skills rather than individual competences. Just as reading aloud has long been a shared practice that nurtures both literacy and emotional connection, co-learning digital skills can create new forms of intergenerational bonding. For example, a parent unfamiliar with online research might sit with their child to evaluate sources together, discussing what makes a website credible or misleading. The child provides agility in navigating the interface; the parent provides the wisdom of scepticism and experience. Such shared moments do not merely close a knowledge gap; they cultivate trust and equip children with critical habits of thought that they might not develop alone. *In this way, the family becomes a micro-classroom where digital discernment is both modelled and practised.*

The benefits extend beyond skills to values. Devices and platforms are not neutral; they embody assumptions about attention, consumption, and social behaviour. Children left to learn in isolation may absorb these uncritically. Parents who co-learn can draw attention to the implicit lessons of digital culture. Why does an app encourage constant notifications? What is gained and what is lost when communication is reduced to emojis or fleeting images? Such conversations are most effective when they emerge from shared exploration rather than top-down lectures. By discovering answers together, parents avoid the common pitfall of appearing out of touch, while children experience guidance as partnership rather than control.

Global examples illustrate both the risks of neglect and the promise of collaboration. In parts of Europe, initiatives have encouraged families to take "digital walks"—sessions where children teach parents to use apps, while parents teach children how to question them. Early evaluations show that children gain a stronger sense of responsibility when positioned as teachers, while parents overcome feelings of incompetence by realising they can still contribute values and context. In contrast, studies from the United States reveal that households where parents simply delegate digital expertise to their children—accepting the narrative that "kids know best"—report higher instances of online risk-taking, from oversharing personal data to exposure to misinformation. The distinction is not in the amount of knowledge parents hold, but in their willingness to engage.

The intergenerational divide is also shaped by socioeconomic context. In wealthier households, parents often outsource digital guidance to tutors, coding camps, or premium platforms, reinforcing children's fluency while simultaneously distancing parents from the process. In lower-income households, parents may lack both the time and confidence to engage, leaving children to learn autonomously. Both extremes perpetuate gaps: one in values transmission, the other in skill acquisition. Co-learning models counter this by requiring minimal resources and emphasising dialogue over expense. A parent who asks, "Show me how you did that," demonstrates interest that transcends financial means. The very act of mutual curiosity becomes a resource, signalling that digital competence is not inherited by class alone but cultivated through shared effort.

Philosophically, bridging the divide challenges us to reconsider authority. Traditional parent–child hierarchies assumed that wisdom flowed downwards: parents knew more, children absorbed. The digital age destabilises this flow, but it need not abolish it. Parents still possess forms of knowledge that technology cannot replace—emotional regulation, ethical reasoning, life experience. The goal is not to compete with children on their ground but to create a partnership where technical fluency and human wisdom reinforce each other. *Authority, in this model, is not about knowing more but about knowing differently.*

There is also a psychological dimension. Many parents confess to feelings of inadequacy when confronted with their children's digital competence. This insecurity can foster avoidance: better to step back than risk embarrassment. But such withdrawal, while understandable, deprives children of guidance they still need. Research consistently shows that young people, though digitally skilled, are not necessarily digitally wise. They know how to operate platforms but struggle to interpret risks, manage attention, or distinguish between authentic and manipulative content. A parent's admission—"I don't know how this works, let's figure it out together"—models humility, resilience, and collaborative problem-solving. These are lessons as valuable as any technical instruction.

Educational systems can amplify or hinder this process. Schools that invite parents into digital literacy programmes, not as passive recipients of training but as co-learners with their children, report stronger outcomes in both family relationships and student performance. In Finland, for instance, family coding workshops have shown that parents often develop confidence not by mastering programming languages but by engaging with their children's problem-solving approaches. In Latin America, community centres that host intergenerational digital storytelling projects reveal similar benefits: children learn to contextualise their digital creativity within family histories, while parents gain tools to participate actively in their children's online worlds. These examples suggest that bridging the divide is not a private task alone but a collective responsibility.

Yet tensions remain. Some parents resist co-learning out of fear that it undermines their authority, while some children bristle at the intrusion of parental presence in spaces they see as private. These tensions are real but can be negotiated. The aim is not constant supervision, which risks turning guidance into policing, but structured engagement. Families that set aside time for joint exploration—whether learning to edit videos, comparing news sources, or experimenting with privacy settings—establish a rhythm of co-learning that respects autonomy while maintaining connection. *The balance lies in presence without suffocation, partnership without surveillance.*

The intergenerational digital divide is not a problem to be solved once but an evolving challenge to be continually renegotiated. As platforms change, so too will the skills required. Today the focus may be on social media and online research; tomorrow it may be on artificial intelligence tools or virtual environments. What remains constant is the need for dialogue, curiosity, and humility across generations. Parents cannot abdicate their role because they are not digital natives, nor should children be left to navigate an algorithmic world alone. The opportunity lies in cultivating a family culture where learning is perpetual and shared, where both generations recognise that expertise is distributed and that wisdom emerges from collaboration.

To bridge the intergenerational divide is not simply to teach parents about apps or children about safety. It is to redefine family life as a partnership in navigating a digital world—one where guidance flows in both directions, authority is reshaped but not abandoned, and learning is a shared responsibility rather than a solitary task.

Chapter 8
Policy Blind Spots

The history of educational reform is littered with well-intentioned but shallow solutions, and few illustrate this more vividly than the digital turn in schools. Over the past two decades, governments across the world have poured billions into technology access initiatives—one laptop per child, tablets for every classroom, broadband subsidies for schools in remote regions. These programmes often make for compelling political announcements, photogenic ribbon-cuttings, and impressive statistics about devices distributed. Yet beneath the surface, the impact on learning outcomes has been far less transformative. *Access alone has never guaranteed understanding, and possession of a device does not equate to the ability to use it critically, creatively, or responsibly.*

The blind spot lies in mistaking infrastructure for pedagogy. Policymakers frequently assume that once the digital barrier is removed, students will naturally flourish. The device becomes a proxy for progress, its presence in the classroom taken as proof of modernisation. But the reality is more sobering. Studies from Latin America's large-scale one-to-one laptop initiatives reveal that without adequate teacher training and curriculum integration, devices quickly became underused or repurposed for entertainment rather than learning. Similarly, in the United States, entire districts have struggled with the unintended consequences of device rollouts—ranging from screen distraction to inequities in home support—because the focus was on acquisition rather than adoption. The political appetite for quick, measurable wins too often overrides the slower, more complex task of cultivating digital literacy and thoughtful teaching practice.

Measurement itself compounds the problem. Standardised testing, already blunt in capturing the richness of learning, becomes even less suited to assessing technology's impact. Policymakers eager to demonstrate returns rely on metrics that privilege quantifiable outputs—such as screen time logged, platforms accessed, or efficiency in test preparation—rather than qualities like critical discernment, sustained attention, or ethical judgement. A school might report high usage rates of a digital platform while students remain vulnerable to misinformation and shallow comprehension. *The danger is that by measuring the wrong things, systems incentivise the wrong behaviours, embedding superficial engagement in place of deeper learning.*

Behind these misalignments lurk the invisible hands of market interests. The educational technology sector, now a multibillion-dollar industry, has become adept at shaping policy agendas to its advantage. Lobbying efforts often emphasise access-based solutions precisely because they align with sales of devices, licences, and platforms. Politicians, seeking visible achievements within electoral cycles, find such proposals attractive: they are easy to fund, distribute, and publicise. The result is a policy landscape where evidence-based pedagogy plays second fiddle to commercial imperatives. The more nuanced questions—how technology should be used, by whom, for what ends, and under what conditions—receive far less attention than the procurement contracts and rollout schedules.

Yet the consequences extend beyond wasted investment. By equating digital equity with device distribution, governments inadvertently reinforce existing inequalities. Wealthier families are able to provide the context missing from policy: digital coaching at home, access to tutors, and supportive environments where critical engagement is modelled. Poorer families, meanwhile, may receive the same device but lack the scaffolding needed to transform it into a genuine learning tool. Instead of narrowing divides, such policies risk widening them, creating a two-tier system in which one group gains enrichment while the other inherits only exposure. *The real divide is not between those who have devices and those who do not, but between those who are taught how to think with them and those who are not.*

Smarter policy design requires reframing the conversation. Devices are not ends in themselves but means to more ambitious goals: equitable learning, empowered teachers, and critical citizens. Governments should be investing less in bulk procurement and more in three underfunded areas: teacher development, curriculum integration, and digital literacy frameworks. Teacher support is especially crucial. Without professional development that equips educators to integrate technology meaningfully, devices become either ornamental or obstructive. Policy needs to acknowledge that the role of the teacher is not diminished but redefined in a digital landscape—they are facilitators of discernment, mediators between student and screen, and curators of learning pathways that algorithms cannot replicate.

Similarly, assessment must evolve. If governments continue to rely on standardised tests as the yardstick, the incentives will remain skewed toward shallow forms of engagement. Alternative evaluation models—portfolio-based assessment, project-driven work, peer-reviewed digital outputs—may be more demanding to implement but better capture the competencies needed in a digital world. Such shifts require political courage, as they are harder to standardise and less immediately quantifiable, but they are essential if policy is to align with the realities of twenty-first-century learning.

There is also the question of accountability. EdTech firms should not be allowed to dictate the agenda unchecked. Independent research, free from commercial influence, must be given greater weight in policy decisions. This requires not only funding for public research bodies but also mechanisms to ensure that pilot projects are evaluated rigorously before being scaled. The temptation to announce large-scale rollouts before evidence has been gathered is strong but must be resisted. *Good policy is less about speed of adoption and more about depth of integration.*

Examples of promising approaches exist. In Estonia, where digital learning outcomes are consistently high, policy has focused less on device distribution and more on teacher training, curriculum redesign, and the integration of coding and digital literacy from an early age. The technology infrastructure is robust, but it is matched by a culture of pedagogical innovation supported by government. In contrast, in parts of sub-Saharan Africa, international initiatives have provided tablets to schools with little follow-up on maintenance, training, or curriculum use, leading to devices that sit unused or become obsolete within years. The comparison underscores a critical point: policy blind spots are not inevitable; they are choices shaped by priorities.

Ultimately, the task for policymakers is to shift from a paradigm of provision to one of cultivation. This means recognising that *the value of technology in education lies not in the number of devices distributed but in the depth of understanding fostered*. It means acknowledging that equity cannot be achieved through hardware alone, but through the ecosystems of support that allow every student to thrive. And it means resisting the lure of market-driven shortcuts in favour of evidence-based, long-term strategies that centre learning rather than consumption.

Policy blind spots will persist as long as technology in education is seen as a matter of supply rather than transformation. To see clearly, governments must be willing to ask harder questions, invest in less visible but more impactful areas, and hold themselves accountable not to industry benchmarks but to the lived experiences of students and teachers. Anything less risks leaving behind not only those without devices, but entire generations unprepared for the complexities of a digital world.

One Device Per Child Isn't Enough

Few policy slogans in the digital education age have carried as much symbolic weight as "one device per child." It captures in four words the alluring promise of equal opportunity through technology: place a laptop or tablet in every student's hands and the path to digital equity will be secured. The idea is so appealing that it has been adopted by governments, NGOs, and corporations alike, becoming shorthand for progress. Yet beneath the rhetorical simplicity lies a far more complex reality. A device, on its own, is not a bridge to digital literacy; it is merely a tool, inert until it is embedded in thoughtful pedagogy, supported by trained teachers, and framed by guidance that encourages critical, ethical, and effective use. *The real challenge is not provision but cultivation, and the failure to recognise this distinction has led to wasted investments, disillusioned educators, and widening inequalities in classrooms around the world.*

The early 2000s saw an explosion of enthusiasm for the "one laptop per child" model, most famously embodied by the eponymous initiative launched by MIT's Nicholas Negroponte. Its bright green laptops, rugged and low-cost, were meant to be revolutionary, bringing millions of children in developing countries into the digital age. Yet the outcomes were mixed at best. Studies in Peru, Uruguay, and Rwanda found that while distribution was extensive, impact on academic achievement was limited. In many cases, the devices were poorly integrated into teaching practice, lacked educational software in local languages, or ended up being used for games rather than structured learning. Teachers reported feeling sidelined, reduced to supervisors of screen time rather than facilitators of knowledge. What these examples underscore is that *access without direction is a fragile foundation for learning.*

Even in wealthier contexts, the equation has not been straightforward. In the United States, large school districts such as Los Angeles spent hundreds of millions of dollars on iPad rollouts, only to face backlash when devices went unused or were repurposed for non-academic activities. Some schools abandoned the initiative entirely, citing low educational returns on a high financial investment. The lesson was clear: technology cannot simply be parachuted into classrooms and expected to generate results. When hardware outpaces human capacity, the gap between potential and practice only widens. *The device is a starting point, not a destination.*

Part of the problem lies in the political attraction of access-based solutions. Devices are tangible, countable, and photogenic. They allow governments to showcase immediate results: hundreds of thousands of tablets distributed, billions invested in digital infrastructure, international accolades for modernisation. Yet these outputs are superficial if they are not matched by investment in teacher training, curriculum redesign, and digital literacy frameworks. The real metrics of success—whether students learn to evaluate information critically, apply digital tools creatively, or navigate ethical dilemmas online—are harder to measure and slower to emerge. In the rush to demonstrate progress, policymakers often overlook the very skills that define meaningful digital engagement.

There is also an equity paradox at play. While universal device programmes are intended to level the playing field, they can inadvertently exacerbate divides. Students from affluent families often receive parental coaching, access to supplemental online resources, and a home environment that models effective digital habits. For them, the school-issued device becomes an extension of a broader ecosystem of support. In contrast, students from disadvantaged backgrounds may receive the same device but lack the scaffolding—whether parental guidance, reliable internet, or quiet study space—that allows it to be used productively. The result is a two-tier outcome: one group advances in both skills and confidence, while the other risks being left behind despite having "equal access." *Digital equality measured in hardware is not the same as digital equity measured in outcomes.*

This is not to dismiss the importance of access altogether. Without devices, no digital learning can take place. The problem arises when access is treated as sufficient in itself, rather than necessary but incomplete. A more nuanced approach recognises that devices are only one piece of a wider puzzle that includes:

- **Teacher capacity**: ensuring educators are not only comfortable with technology but trained to integrate it meaningfully into lesson design.
- **Curriculum relevance**: aligning digital tools with learning objectives rather than treating them as add-ons.
- **Critical literacy**: embedding instruction in how to navigate information, resist manipulation, and use technology responsibly.
- **Contextual adaptation**: providing software and content in local languages and cultural frameworks, avoiding the one-size-fits-all approach that privileges English-dominated platforms.

These elements are harder to fund, harder to measure, and harder to market than a device rollout, but they are indispensable if digital initiatives are to translate into real learning gains.

Consider the contrasting trajectories of Uruguay's Plan Ceibal and India's tablet distribution schemes. Uruguay invested heavily not just in devices but in teacher training, local content development, and ongoing evaluation. Over time, this holistic model has shown more promising outcomes, with improvements in student engagement and the integration of digital practices across subjects. India, by contrast, focused largely on the hardware, distributing millions of tablets without equivalent support systems. The result was high rates of underuse and limited impact on student performance. The divergence illustrates a fundamental principle: *technology magnifies existing capacities—it does not substitute for their absence.*

The deeper issue is philosophical as much as practical. By equating education with access to devices, we risk reducing learning to a transactional encounter between student and screen. This overlooks the relational and interpretive dimensions of education: the role of dialogue, mentorship, and critical questioning that no device can replicate. The vision of a student autonomously learning simply because they hold a laptop is not only unrealistic but also impoverished. It strips education of its social and human elements, recasting it as an individualised consumption of content rather than a shared process of meaning-making. The device-centred paradigm appeals to a certain technocratic mindset but fails to capture the richness of what learning entails.

This blind spot persists because it is easier to provide devices than to transform systems. It requires less political capital to announce a procurement programme than to overhaul assessment frameworks, retrain teachers, or confront entrenched inequalities. Yet the cost of avoiding these deeper reforms is borne by students who graduate digitally connected but cognitively underprepared. They may have mastered the mechanics of swiping, typing, and searching, but not the intellectual resilience needed to discern credible sources, sustain attention, or create new knowledge. In the long run, societies that confuse access with understanding will find themselves with populations that are connected but not empowered.

The real question, then, is not how to give every child a device, but how to ensure that every child acquires the *capacity to learn with a device*. That capacity is cultivated not through one-off rollouts but through sustained investment in ecosystems of guidance. Teachers must be positioned as facilitators of digital discernment rather than passive monitors of device use. Parents must be included as partners, provided with resources to support their children's digital engagement at home. Curricula must shift from rote memorisation to inquiry-based models that harness technology as a tool for exploration rather than distraction. Without these, the rhetoric of "one device per child" risks becoming an expensive distraction from the harder but more transformative work of building digital literacy.

To move beyond access, policymakers, educators, and communities must embrace a simple but often overlooked truth: *technology is not self-executing*. It acquires educational power only when embedded in human structures of guidance, mentorship, and critical reflection. A laptop can be a window to the world, but it can also be a mirror of inequality. The distinction depends not on the device itself but on the ecosystem in which it is placed. To imagine otherwise is to fall for the illusion that tools alone can teach.

Testing, Data, and the Wrong Metrics

One of the most striking contradictions in contemporary education policy is the mismatch between the sophistication of the technologies entering classrooms and the crudity of the tools used to measure their impact. Around the world, school systems trumpet investments in laptops, tablets, interactive platforms, and digital curricula. They speak of "future-ready learners" and "twenty-first-century skills." Yet when the time comes to evaluate whether these innovations have borne fruit, the assessment still largely revolves around standardised tests of reading and mathematics—metrics designed for another age, incapable of capturing the complexities of digital learning. The result is a profound disconnect: students are taught in environments increasingly shaped by algorithms, platforms, and online networks, but their progress is measured by instruments that cannot register critical thinking, creativity, collaboration, or digital literacy. *This misalignment distorts policy, frustrates teachers, and leaves societies blind to the deeper markers of genuine learning.*

Standardised testing remains appealing to policymakers for obvious reasons: it is quantifiable, comparable, and convenient. A government minister can point to improved test scores as evidence of progress, or to a global ranking as validation of reform. The simplicity of such metrics provides a narrative of control in a complex system. Yet the price of this simplicity is that the most essential skills for thriving in a digital society are rendered invisible. No multiple-choice exam captures whether a student can discern misinformation, weigh ethical trade-offs in technology use, or collaborate across digital platforms to solve problems. These are not luxuries; they are the very competencies that determine whether access to devices translates into empowerment or exploitation. *By measuring the wrong things, we risk teaching the wrong things.*

Research illustrates the danger of this fixation. For instance, studies of large-scale laptop rollouts in Latin America showed minimal improvements in test scores despite significant investments in technology. Critics seized on these results as proof that digital initiatives "do not work." But the tests themselves were narrowly designed to measure traditional literacy and numeracy, not the broader dimensions of digital engagement. The absence of measurable gains said as much about the limits of the evaluation framework as about the initiatives themselves. Similarly, in the United States, debates over "screen time" often hinge on whether technology improves performance on standardised exams, as though these were the ultimate indicators of success. In reality, students may develop resilience in navigating online environments, creativity in multimedia expression, or fluency in coding—skills unlikely to register on reading comprehension tests but vital for modern economies.

The inadequacy of current metrics also warps classroom practice. Teachers, under pressure to produce results that are legible to policymakers, may avoid integrating technology in innovative ways if those methods do not clearly improve test scores. Instead of experimenting with project-based learning, collaborative digital inquiry, or creative media production, they may revert to "drill and practice" software that mimics traditional worksheets in digital form. These platforms often do produce modest test-score gains, since they align neatly with assessment content, but they also reinforce a reductive vision of learning that treats students as data points rather than thinkers. *In effect, the testing regime rewards the least ambitious uses of technology while penalising the more transformative possibilities.*

Contrast this with alternative assessment models being piloted in places like Finland or Singapore, where education systems have experimented with broader indicators of learning. In Finland, schools have increasingly adopted cross-disciplinary projects where students use digital tools to investigate real-world problems, with assessments focused on process as well as outcome. Singapore has invested in frameworks that assess collaborative problem-solving and adaptability, recognising these as essential competencies for the future workforce. These systems are not flawless, but they represent attempts to measure what matters rather than what is easy. They remind us that metrics are not neutral: they embody values. Choosing to measure only test scores signals that we value narrow knowledge reproduction; choosing to measure critical literacy, creativity, and ethical reasoning signals a very different vision of education.

There is also a political economy to testing that cannot be ignored. Standardised assessment is a multi-billion-dollar industry, dominated by a handful of corporations whose interests are not always aligned with the cultivation of rich learning environments. The expansion of digital testing platforms has only deepened their influence. EdTech companies often market software that promises improved test results, reinforcing the primacy of outdated metrics. Policymakers, eager for evidence of success, embrace these solutions without questioning whether the metrics themselves are appropriate. The cycle perpetuates itself: narrow measures lead to narrow tools, which in turn validate narrow learning outcomes. *Data becomes a substitute for wisdom.*

To break this cycle, we need to reconsider what counts as evidence in education. Raw test scores offer a thin slice of information, often stripped of context and insensitive to equity. More meaningful indicators might include whether students can collaborate across cultural and linguistic divides online, whether they demonstrate resilience in tackling complex problems without clear solutions, or whether they can critically evaluate the algorithms shaping their information environments. These are harder to measure, but not impossible. Portfolios, peer assessments, reflective writing, and project-based evaluations can all provide richer insights into how students are actually thinking and applying knowledge. Digital tools themselves can be leveraged to track process as well as product, capturing not only the final answer but the pathways taken to reach it.

Critics may argue that such assessments lack comparability or rigour. Yet the pursuit of perfect comparability has already led us into an impoverished conception of learning. The alternative is not an abandonment of rigour but a redefinition of it—away from the illusion of objectivity provided by standardised tests and towards a more holistic, nuanced, and context-sensitive understanding of student growth. In medicine, we would never assess the health of a patient using only a single measure, such as blood pressure. Education deserves the same multidimensionality.

The problem of wrong metrics extends beyond the classroom into how societies evaluate the success of entire education systems. International comparisons such as PISA dominate headlines, yet their emphasis on reading, maths, and science narrows the discourse about what good education entails. Countries may adjust curricula simply to perform better on these tests, even if doing so undermines local needs or cultural values. When technology initiatives are judged primarily by their effect on PISA scores, the result is a distortion of priorities. Investments in critical digital literacy, for example, may be neglected because they do not directly boost test performance, even though they are essential for democratic resilience in an age of misinformation. *What we measure ends up shaping what we become.*

At the heart of this issue lies a philosophical tension: is education about transmitting knowledge or cultivating wisdom? Knowledge is easier to test; wisdom resists quantification. Yet it is wisdom—judgement, discernment, the capacity to connect dots across contexts—that defines whether students can navigate the digital world responsibly and creatively. By clinging to outdated metrics, we risk producing students who can pass exams but cannot evaluate an online conspiracy theory, who can solve textbook problems but cannot adapt to real-world complexity. This is not merely an academic concern; it has consequences for economies, democracies, and civic life.

If the current moment teaches anything, it is that education systems must learn to measure what matters, even if doing so is messier, slower, and less headline-grabbing than test-score improvements. Devices in classrooms are not ends in themselves but catalysts for new forms of thinking. Unless assessments evolve to reflect this reality, we will remain trapped in a paradox where the presence of technology suggests progress while the metrics used to evaluate it conceal stagnation. The future of education depends not only on the tools we adopt but also on the measures we choose to guide them. To cling to the wrong metrics is to risk mistaking motion for movement, activity for achievement, access for understanding. Only by reimagining how we evaluate learning can we hope to see clearly what technology is truly contributing to the lives of students.

EdTech Lobbying and Market Interests

The story of educational technology is often framed as one of progress: innovative tools sweeping into classrooms, democratising access, and modernising learning. Yet behind this narrative lies another, less discussed but equally important one—the growing influence of commercial interests in shaping how education policy is written and enacted. Far from being a neutral marketplace of ideas, the EdTech sector has become a powerful lobbying force whose interests do not always align with the pedagogical needs of students or the professional realities of teachers. *When profit motives intersect with public education, policy risks being guided less by evidence and more by marketing imperatives.*

The sheer scale of investment in EdTech over the past two decades has created conditions for intense lobbying. By 2022, global expenditure on education technology had surpassed $250 billion annually, with projections of continued growth. For venture capital firms and multinational corporations, schools are not just sites of learning but markets. Devices, apps, learning platforms, and data systems all represent revenue streams. In such a climate, companies cannot afford to leave adoption to chance. Lobbying—whether through direct political engagement, partnerships with ministries, or influence on philanthropic initiatives—becomes a central strategy. The result is a subtle but profound distortion: decisions about which technologies to adopt, and on what scale, are frequently shaped by the strength of corporate persuasion rather than by independent evidence of effectiveness.

Consider the case of one-to-one laptop initiatives, which spread rapidly in the 2000s across North America, Europe, and Latin America. Promoted as transformative, these programmes were heavily championed by hardware manufacturers keen to secure long-term contracts with governments. While some contexts saw benefits, evidence on learning outcomes was mixed at best, with many initiatives failing to provide adequate teacher training or curricular integration. Nonetheless, the programmes proliferated, largely because policymakers were convinced by the appeal of visible, quantifiable investments: a device in every student's hands. This mirrored the interests of the technology companies supplying the devices far more than the nuanced realities of classroom learning. *Here, lobbying succeeded in equating access with progress, narrowing the scope of educational debate.*

Another dimension of influence lies in how EdTech firms shape the language of policy. Concepts such as "personalised learning," "data-driven decision-making," and "future-ready skills" have become buzzwords in government documents worldwide. Yet these terms often originate in corporate marketing strategies rather than in educational research. For example, adaptive learning platforms are sold with the promise of tailoring content to individual student needs, a claim that resonates with policymakers seeking efficiency and equity. But the empirical evidence for such tools improving long-term learning outcomes remains limited. What is marketed as innovation may in fact be a repackaging of drill-and-practice methods, now delivered with glossy interfaces and extensive data collection. The rhetoric of transformation obscures the reality of continuity.

This raises another concern: the commodification of student data. Many EdTech platforms rely on gathering vast amounts of information on student behaviour, performance, and engagement. These data are presented as essential for improving learning outcomes, but they also serve commercial purposes—informing product development, driving targeted marketing, or even being monetised in ways opaque to schools and families. Policymakers, often under pressure to embrace digitalisation, may not scrutinise the long-term implications of these practices. Lobbyists present data collection as a natural component of twenty-first-century learning, framing scepticism as resistance to progress. Yet the ethical stakes are high: students, the least empowered actors in the system, become both consumers and products in an economy of surveillance.

The influence of EdTech lobbying is not always overt. Sometimes it takes the form of corporate partnerships with governments, in which companies provide free tools or platforms to schools in exchange for long-term dependency. During the COVID-19 pandemic, for instance, platforms like Google Classroom and Microsoft Teams rapidly entrenched themselves in school systems, often at no initial cost. While this ensured continuity of learning, it also locked institutions into ecosystems where exit becomes difficult, given the training, integration, and reliance that develop over time. The "freemium" model—free at the point of adoption, expensive once entrenched—has proven a powerful lever for corporate influence. What looks like philanthropy is often a market-capture strategy.

There are, of course, counterarguments. Some contend that corporate innovation is essential in education, as governments and public systems lack the capacity to develop cutting-edge tools at scale. From this perspective, lobbying is not inherently malign but part of a dynamic ecosystem where private and public actors collaborate to drive progress. Certainly, many technological advances—such as accessible online resources, communication tools, or assistive technologies for students with disabilities—owe much to private sector investment. Yet the crucial distinction lies in whether policy is guided by evidence-based pedagogy or by the imperatives of market expansion. *Innovation becomes problematic when it dictates educational priorities rather than serving them.*

The political economy of EdTech also reveals stark global inequities. In the Global South, governments under pressure to modernise may adopt technologies promoted by multinational firms without sufficient attention to local contexts. A platform designed for English-speaking students in affluent systems may be ill-suited to multilingual, resource-constrained classrooms. Yet lobbying campaigns often gloss over these mismatches, promising universal solutions to deeply contextual challenges. When policies fail to deliver, it is the students—not the companies—that bear the cost. The structural imbalance of power between global corporations and local education ministries exacerbates dependency and weakens the autonomy of education systems.

Philanthropy adds another layer of complexity. Foundations linked to technology billionaires often shape education agendas through funding and advocacy, framing themselves as neutral benefactors while advancing models aligned with corporate interests. Initiatives such as providing devices, sponsoring research, or developing new curricula may bring real resources, but they also steer policy conversations in particular directions—often privileging technological solutions over structural reforms in teacher training, curriculum development, or equity of access. The line between altruism and market preparation is increasingly blurred.

To navigate these dynamics, governments must develop greater critical literacy in engaging with EdTech. Transparency about lobbying efforts should be mandatory, with disclosures of corporate influence on policy design. Independent, peer-reviewed research needs to take precedence over white papers commissioned by vendors. Procurement processes should evaluate not just cost and scale but also pedagogical alignment, ethical considerations, and long-term sustainability. Some countries have begun experimenting with national frameworks for EdTech adoption that emphasise evidence and equity. Such frameworks represent attempts to reclaim agency from markets and re-centre policy around learning rather than lobbying.

The stakes are not trivial. Education is not a typical marketplace where consumer choice regulates quality. It is a public good, shaping the intellectual and civic capacities of entire generations. Allowing policy to be driven primarily by commercial agendas risks narrowing the possibilities of learning to what is profitable rather than what is pedagogically sound. The most effective technologies may not be the most lucrative; the most equitable policies may not be the most marketable. Recognising this tension is essential if societies are to avoid mistaking corporate ambition for educational progress.

The deeper issue is philosophical: do we see students as citizens to be cultivated or as consumers to be captured? The former requires policies rooted in pedagogy, equity, and critical literacy; the latter invites an uncritical embrace of platforms that promise efficiency and scale. The challenge is not to reject technology but to resist ceding control of education to the logics of the market. If technology is to serve learning rather than the other way around, policymakers must learn to hear beyond the lobbying—asking not only what is profitable but what is just, not only what is efficient but what is transformative. Only then can education escape the gravitational pull of commercial interests and remain oriented towards its deeper purpose: preparing individuals and societies to think, question, and act with wisdom in a complex world.

Toward Smarter Policy Design

For decades, the dominant reflex of education policy in the face of digital inequality has been to purchase more devices. Governments, under pressure to demonstrate progress, frequently default to visible, quantifiable initiatives: laptops in every classroom, tablets distributed en masse, connectivity schemes rolled out across districts. Yet history has shown that these measures, while symbolically powerful, are insufficient when left unaccompanied by deeper investment in pedagogy, teacher support, and critical literacy. *Equitable access is not achieved merely by distributing hardware; it is sustained only when infrastructure is matched with capacity, training, and the cultivation of discerning digital citizens.*

The problem lies partly in the nature of political incentives. Devices are politically legible: a minister can hold a press conference and point to thousands of tablets deployed as evidence of progress. But the subtler, less photogenic dimensions of education—teacher development, student engagement, the fostering of critical thinking—do not lend themselves to ribbon-cutting ceremonies. Consequently, policymaking often prioritises what is visible over what is transformative. This imbalance must be corrected if digital learning is to support equity rather than deepen divides.

Smarter policy design begins with recognising that access is necessary but not sufficient. The first generation of large-scale initiatives, from Uruguay's Plan Ceibal to India's Aakash tablet project, revealed the dangers of equating devices with learning. In both cases, the provision of technology outpaced the ability of teachers and students to integrate it meaningfully into the learning process. Where comprehensive training, curricular adaptation, and ongoing support were absent, devices became underused, misused, or abandoned altogether. *The central insight here is that the value of technology depends less on its presence than on the social, cultural, and pedagogical ecosystems into which it is introduced.*

Teacher support is arguably the most neglected pillar of digital education policy. Teachers are often positioned as passive recipients of new tools rather than as active partners in shaping how those tools are deployed. This dynamic reflects a technocratic assumption: that software and hardware, by themselves, can generate outcomes. In reality, the most successful digital learning environments are those where teachers are empowered to adapt technology to their pedagogical goals. Finland provides a telling example. Its approach has consistently emphasised teacher autonomy and professional development, ensuring that technology is framed as an aid to pedagogical creativity rather than a rigid system imposed from above. Contrast this with the rollout of interactive whiteboards in many English schools during the early 2000s, which were often used as glorified projectors because teachers had not been given the training or time to integrate them effectively. Investment in teacher capacity determines whether technology becomes an enabler or a distraction.

Alongside professional development, equity must be addressed not just at the level of hardware but also in terms of context. A rural school without reliable electricity cannot benefit from the same digital solutions as an urban school with high-speed broadband. Similarly, learners who speak minority languages are poorly served by platforms built exclusively in English. Policy design must therefore attend to the specificities of local environments, resisting the allure of one-size-fits-all solutions marketed by global vendors. This means funding not only infrastructure but also localisation efforts, community-based initiatives, and research into culturally responsive digital pedagogies. *Equity is never a static target; it requires ongoing adaptation to local realities and shifting forms of exclusion.*

Another cornerstone of smarter policy lies in cultivating critical digital literacy among students. The danger of equating digital inclusion with device access is that it reduces learners to mere users rather than active interpreters of technology. A student with a tablet but without the skills to discern misinformation, evaluate sources, or understand algorithmic bias is digitally connected but not digitally empowered. Policy, therefore, must fund curricula that integrate media literacy, ethical reasoning, and civic engagement into digital learning programmes. Some countries, such as Sweden, have made strides in embedding media literacy across subjects, recognising that critical engagement with technology is as important as technical proficiency. Without this dimension, digital education risks producing compliant consumers rather than thoughtful citizens.

Funding frameworks should also prioritise sustainability over spectacle. Too often, pilot projects are launched with great fanfare, only to falter once the initial funding cycle ends. Sustainable design means investing in ongoing maintenance, iterative evaluation, and the capacity for schools to evolve alongside technology. Chile's Enlaces programme offers a model here: beginning in the 1990s, it adopted a long-term vision of gradual integration, combining infrastructure with teacher training, curriculum support, and monitoring. Its endurance, compared to short-lived device-distribution projects elsewhere, highlights the value of policy patience and systemic investment.

Yet designing smarter policy also requires confronting the power dynamics of the EdTech market. Governments are frequently courted by corporations whose interests lie in maximising sales and market share rather than educational outcomes. To counterbalance this, procurement processes must be restructured to privilege evidence-based solutions, interoperability, and ethical safeguards over vendor lock-in. Open-source platforms and public investment in home-grown solutions deserve greater support, both to foster local innovation and to reduce dependency on global monopolies. Public policy should resist the framing of technology as a product to be consumed and instead treat it as a public infrastructure to be cultivated.

Accountability is essential. Too often, digital initiatives are launched without clear benchmarks for measuring success beyond crude indicators such as device numbers or log-in rates. Smarter frameworks would evaluate technology's impact on deeper learning markers: critical thinking, collaboration, problem-solving, and long-term retention. This requires designing new assessment tools that go beyond standardised tests to capture how technology reshapes the learning process. Singapore's policy approach is instructive: its ICT Masterplans have consistently emphasised pedagogy-driven use of technology, with rigorous monitoring mechanisms that prioritise outcomes over optics.

At the philosophical level, smarter policy design asks governments to reframe their responsibility. Education cannot be outsourced to technology companies, nor can it be reduced to metrics of efficiency. The role of policy is to protect the public character of education: to ensure that technology serves human development, equity, and civic participation rather than market expansion. This means embedding safeguards for privacy, insisting on transparency in data use, and foregrounding ethical considerations in every procurement decision. In an era where digital ecosystems are increasingly shaped by profit motives, public policy must act as a counterbalance, keeping pedagogy and equity at the centre.

Ultimately, the design of digital education policy is a test of political imagination. It is easy to count devices; it is harder to measure wisdom. The real task for policymakers is to move beyond symbolic gestures and build frameworks that invest in teachers, foster critical literacy, adapt to diverse contexts, and resist commercial capture. *Smarter policy is not about doing more with technology but about asking better questions of it—what purposes it serves, whose interests it advances, and how it can deepen rather than diminish the possibilities of education.* If governments can rise to this challenge, digital learning can evolve from a series of disconnected experiments into a coherent, equitable, and enduring public good.

Chapter 9
Rethinking Digital Equity

Equity in digital education is too often conflated with equality, as though handing out the same device or providing the same internet package automatically levels the playing field. The reality, borne out across classrooms, households, and communities worldwide, is that *equal inputs do not translate into equal outcomes*. A child in a household where parents can guide them through online resources, contextualise misinformation, and cultivate healthy study routines will not experience technology in the same way as a child left to navigate the digital sphere unsupported. The assumption that sameness creates fairness obscures the deeper challenge: equity requires differentiation, adaptation, and sensitivity to the specific barriers each learner faces.

The danger of policies and programmes built around equality rather than equity is that they are blind to context. A rural learner provided with a laptop but no reliable broadband is not in the same position as an urban peer who has stable internet and a parent with digital expertise. A student who speaks the dominant language of platforms has an inbuilt advantage over one who must wrestle with poorly translated materials or whose linguistic community is ignored altogether. When governments and organisations measure progress simply by counting devices distributed or connections established, they risk mistaking inputs for outcomes. The reality is that technology amplifies advantage as much as it mitigates disadvantage. Unless support is tailored, the gaps widen.

Some of the most meaningful experiments in digital equity do not come from ministries of education or Silicon Valley boardrooms but from community spaces where innovation is grounded in lived realities. Libraries, community centres, and grassroots NGOs have long acted as bridges for those excluded from formal pathways of access. A public library in Toronto that offers coding clubs for immigrant youth, a community hall in Nairobi that doubles as a Wi-Fi hub for schoolchildren, or an NGO in rural Bangladesh equipping women with digital literacy skills—all of these examples highlight the same principle: equity must be embedded in context, not delivered as a uniform package. These initiatives succeed not because they offer cutting-edge hardware but because they cultivate trust, accessibility, and support structures that mainstream policy often overlooks.

What is striking about these community-led models is their flexibility. They recognise that the barriers to digital learning are not only technical but social and cultural. In low-resource settings, peer mentorship often becomes the most powerful equaliser. Young people frequently learn more effectively from those only slightly ahead of them on the digital curve than from distant experts. A teenager who has figured out how to navigate a learning app becomes a local tutor for peers; a group of students teaches one another basic coding skills, multiplying knowledge horizontally. *Peer-to-peer learning not only spreads skills efficiently but also fosters confidence, belonging, and the sense that technology is not the preserve of elites but something ordinary people can master together.*

These dynamics matter because they disrupt the myth of digital fluency as an individual trait. In reality, digital learning is profoundly social. Skills are borrowed, adapted, and shared. Communities with strong peer networks can overcome resource gaps that would otherwise cripple progress. Conversely, communities without such networks may find that even with devices, learners remain isolated, uncertain, or overwhelmed. Recognising peer mentorship as an essential part of digital equity reframes the problem: the goal is not just to provide access but to cultivate ecosystems of mutual support.

To move toward a meaningful framework for digital equity, interventions must combine four elements: access, literacy, guidance, and adaptability. Access ensures the basic infrastructure—devices, connectivity, platforms—without which participation is impossible. Literacy encompasses not only technical skills but also critical capacities: discerning misinformation, understanding data privacy, and navigating online risks. Guidance recognises the role of parents, teachers, and mentors in scaffolding learning and helping young people use technology with intention rather than drift. Adaptability ensures that interventions are sensitive to local contexts, languages, and cultural norms, rather than imposing universal solutions designed elsewhere. *Only when these dimensions operate together can digital equity become more than an empty promise.*

This requires a shift in how policymakers, educators, and funders conceptualise success. Counting log-ins or measuring device ratios cannot capture the richness—or the failures—of digital learning. Instead, success must be assessed by whether learners can engage meaningfully with technology, apply it to their own goals, and participate fully in civic, economic, and cultural life. Real equity will often look uneven: some learners will need more support than others, some communities will require deeper investment, and some systems will evolve at different paces. The aim is not to erase difference but to ensure that difference does not calcify into exclusion.

The challenge of rethinking digital equity is therefore both philosophical and practical. Philosophically, it demands that we abandon the seductive illusion that technology is neutral or self-levelling. Practically, it calls for policies and practices that are slower, more context-driven, and less obsessed with scale for its own sake. Community-level initiatives, peer-to-peer networks, differentiated support models—all of these are harder to measure than device counts, but they are closer to the reality of how equity is built. *The future of digital learning will depend less on how many tools are distributed than on how wisely, inclusively, and imaginatively they are used.*

This chapter begins from that recognition and pushes beyond it, offering a roadmap for how societies can rethink what equity means in the digital age. It asks what it would take to design systems that honour diversity rather than erase it, that prioritise guidance over policing, collaboration over competition, and critical literacy over passive consumption. In doing so, it argues for nothing less than a reframing of digital education—not as a question of closing a gap with uniform inputs, but as the ongoing, collective work of ensuring that technology serves as a bridge rather than a boundary.

Equity Beyond Equality

For decades, policymakers and educators have clung to a deceptively simple formula: if every child has the same tool, then every child has the same opportunity. Laptops distributed en masse, tablets issued by school districts, or subsidised internet plans rolled out by governments are often presented as solutions to the digital divide. Yet the persistence—and in many cases, deepening—of disparities in educational outcomes reveals the flaw at the heart of this logic. *Equality of distribution is not equity of experience.* Technology does not float in a vacuum; it interacts with a learner's environment, support structures, and prior knowledge. To treat access alone as the marker of fairness is to overlook the reality that what matters most is not sameness but differentiation—support that recognises where learners start, what resources surround them, and how guidance shapes their ability to use tools meaningfully.

The distinction between equality and equity is not merely semantic. Equality implies uniform provision: every student receives the same device, the same online curriculum, the same set of passwords and log-ins. Equity, however, acknowledges variation. It recognises that a child living in a crowded household without a quiet corner to study will not benefit from a laptop in the same way as a peer with their own desk and a parent able to troubleshoot technical issues. It recognises that learners who struggle with literacy need scaffolded digital resources, not just a portal of text-heavy assignments. Equity demands *responsiveness*—policies and practices that adjust to circumstances rather than pretending those circumstances do not matter.

Consider the well-publicised "One Laptop per Child" initiative, launched in the mid-2000s with the utopian promise of bridging global educational divides. Millions of inexpensive laptops were distributed to schools across the Global South. The symbolic power of the programme was immense, but follow-up evaluations found disappointing results. Many devices were left unused, broken, or diverted for other purposes. Teachers often lacked training to integrate them into lessons, and parents, unfamiliar with digital tools, could not provide at-home support. The project highlighted a crucial lesson: *technology without context is inert.* Access may open the door, but it does not teach children to walk through it, much less guide them along the path.

Contrast this with smaller, localised programmes where differentiated support is central. In parts of India, NGOs have experimented with "digital plus mentoring" schemes, pairing tablet distribution with weekly tutoring sessions that help children and parents alike navigate content. In these communities, outcomes have been strikingly better than device-only rollouts. Learners not only engage more consistently but also demonstrate improved comprehension and critical thinking. What differentiates these models is not the technology itself but the scaffolding around it: literacy support, contextualised teaching, and relational guidance. *Equity is not just about giving more to those with less, but about tailoring interventions so they make sense in the specific ecosystem of each learner's life.*

This principle applies just as powerfully in wealthy nations. When schools in the United States or the United Kingdom rushed to adopt one-to-one laptop schemes, they often discovered that students from higher-income households used devices for research, project-based learning, and creative expression, while those from lower-income households gravitated toward entertainment or struggled with basic navigation. The same machine became, in effect, two different tools. Without targeted teaching, critical digital literacy, and parental engagement, the promise of equal devices turned into the reality of unequal outcomes. This mirrors the long-observed "Matthew effect" in education: those with prior advantages accumulate more from each additional resource, while those without are left further behind.

Why, then, does the rhetoric of equality persist? Partly because it is administratively tidy. Equality is easy to measure: one device per child, one hotspot per household, one login per student. Equity is harder, because it requires nuanced indicators and long-term monitoring. It demands that policymakers ask uncomfortable questions about the lived realities of children, families, and teachers—questions that often expose structural inequalities beyond the classroom. Moreover, equality is politically appealing. A minister who announces a universal device distribution programme can claim tangible progress; the subtler work of ensuring those devices are embedded in supportive ecosystems rarely makes headlines.

Yet the stakes of ignoring equity are high. The illusion that equality is sufficient masks the reproduction of advantage. If affluent families can supplement school-provided devices with coding camps, digital tutors, and parental guidance, while disadvantaged families cannot, the gap grows wider even though, on paper, access has been equalised. Worse, the rhetoric of equality allows institutions to deflect responsibility: once devices are handed out, failures of engagement are attributed to students or families rather than to the inadequacy of support. The risk is a cycle in which *the very interventions designed to close the divide end up entrenching it further.*

Reframing the conversation toward equity requires a shift in mindset at multiple levels. At the policy level, funding must prioritise not only infrastructure but also the human supports that make infrastructure meaningful: teacher training, parent workshops, multilingual resources, and culturally sensitive curricula. At the school level, leaders must recognise that digital learning is not uniform; it requires adaptation to learners with diverse needs. At the community level, NGOs, libraries, and local mentors play a vital role in filling the gaps that universal policies inevitably leave. In all of these contexts, the critical question is not "Does every child have a device?" but "Does every child have the conditions to use that device productively?"

Some education thinkers argue that equity should be understood less as a static goal and more as a continuous process. Needs shift over time: a primary school pupil requires different digital supports than a teenager preparing for higher education; a community with intermittent connectivity has different priorities than one where the issue is not access but attention management. Equity, in this sense, is not a box to be ticked but a practice of constant recalibration. *Fairness lies not in treating everyone the same but in treating each learner with the recognition that their context demands something specific.*

Philosophically, this distinction forces us to confront our assumptions about justice in education. The egalitarian impulse is powerful, and rightly so: every child deserves dignity, resources, and opportunity. But dignity is not preserved by pretending that identical treatment yields identical outcomes. True justice recognises difference, embraces complexity, and allocates resources in ways that may appear uneven but are in fact more just. In education, this means designing systems that anticipate disparity rather than react to it belatedly.

In practice, this might involve policies that direct more support to schools serving disadvantaged populations, even if device distribution is already universal. It might mean embedding critical digital literacy into curricula from the earliest years, ensuring that children do not simply consume digital content but learn to question, evaluate, and create. It could involve partnerships with parents that acknowledge their own gaps in digital confidence, transforming them from passive monitors into active co-learners with their children. The point is not to design perfect uniformity but to cultivate resilience and agency across diverse contexts.

The task, then, is to move beyond the comfort of equality toward the more demanding, more honest pursuit of equity. To do so requires courage: the courage to acknowledge that simple solutions rarely address complex realities, that fairness is not sameness, and that justice in digital education is measured not by distribution counts but by lived outcomes. If equality was the rallying cry of the early digital divide debates, equity must become the watchword of the next phase. It is the difference between handing out tools and ensuring those tools build futures. It is the difference between access and agency. And it is, ultimately, the difference between a digital education system that perpetuates privilege and one that truly expands opportunity.

Bridging Gaps at Community Level

If governments and education systems often stumble in their efforts to deliver meaningful digital equity, community-level actors have quietly been crafting some of the most impactful responses to the digital divide. It is frequently in libraries, local NGOs, and community centres that innovation flourishes—not in the form of expensive hardware rollouts or sweeping policy proclamations, but through small-scale, human-centred interventions designed to meet learners where they are. These spaces remind us that digital equity is not merely a national policy problem but a lived, local one; it is shaped by context, trust, and relationships. And while policymakers debate metrics, community institutions are already redefining what it means to provide meaningful access.

Libraries are perhaps the most underappreciated players in the struggle for digital literacy. Once dismissed by some as relics of the print era, libraries have instead transformed into hubs for digital learning. In countless towns and cities, they provide not only free internet and computers but also staff who act as informal digital coaches. The significance of this cannot be overstated. A public library is often one of the few places where a teenager without Wi-Fi at home can complete assignments, or where an adult seeking to re-enter the workforce can learn how to create an email address, navigate job portals, or update a CV. *Libraries demonstrate that access is inseparable from guidance: it is the librarian's patient coaching, not just the keyboard or the Wi-Fi, that unlocks opportunity.* During the COVID-19 pandemic, some libraries in the United States even kept their Wi-Fi on 24/7 so that students could sit outside the building to complete homework. Such actions illustrate how deeply embedded these institutions are in their communities, and how their flexibility allows them to respond swiftly to crises in ways that national systems rarely manage.

Community centres, too, play a crucial role, particularly in areas where schools cannot bridge the gap alone. In parts of sub-Saharan Africa, centres run by NGOs have become lifelines for young learners. These centres often provide solar-powered computer labs where electricity is unreliable, or low-bandwidth offline servers hosting open educational resources for communities without steady internet connections. Importantly, these spaces do not just provide tools; they provide environments where learners can practice, fail, and try again under the guidance of mentors who understand their context. A child in rural Kenya may not have parents with the skills to help them navigate digital platforms, but at a local centre they might encounter a facilitator who introduces them to coding games, digital storytelling tools, or safe browsing practices. What is being taught is not simply how to click and type but how to imagine oneself as a participant in the digital world.

NGOs, unburdened by the bureaucracy that often slows formal education systems, are able to innovate in nimble and context-sensitive ways. Consider the work of organisations like Code Club in the United Kingdom, which organises volunteers to run after-school coding sessions in libraries and community halls. These sessions demystify programming and present it as something accessible and creative rather than elite and intimidating. Or take the case of Pratham in India, which has experimented with blended learning models in rural communities, combining face-to-face teaching with carefully structured digital interventions delivered on tablets. Their focus is not on flashy technology but on incremental literacy gains, using digital tools to complement rather than replace local educators. Such initiatives succeed not because they hand out devices, but because they embed those devices in webs of mentorship, guidance, and practice.

A striking feature of community-level interventions is their recognition of the social dimension of digital learning. Where large-scale access programmes often imagine the learner as an isolated individual with a device, community efforts see learning as relational. At a library, a group of students may cluster around a single screen, sharing ideas and teaching one another. In a community centre, adults and children may learn side by side, breaking down intergenerational divides in digital fluency. NGOs often recruit local youth as peer mentors, creating ripple effects as knowledge circulates outward. *The genius of community-level work lies in its ability to convert digital literacy from a solitary act into a shared culture.* This matters, because it ensures that learning is reinforced not only by the technology itself but also by the networks of support that surround it.

Of course, community-level solutions are not free from limitations. Libraries in many countries struggle with funding cuts, leaving them with outdated equipment or reduced opening hours. NGOs often rely on short-term grants, which means promising projects disappear when funding cycles end. Community centres in under-resourced areas may be overwhelmed by demand, unable to serve everyone who needs them. These constraints highlight an uncomfortable truth: while community initiatives are indispensable, they cannot be left to fill systemic gaps indefinitely. Their successes should not excuse governments from building long-term infrastructure, but rather serve as models to be scaled and supported.

At the same time, there is something important about the *localness* of these interventions that should not be lost in the rush to scale. Equity is context-sensitive; what works in a London library may not translate to a rural Ghanaian village, and what succeeds in an urban Indian slum may be irrelevant in a remote Canadian First Nations community. Community-led efforts succeed precisely because they are tailored to their contexts. They draw on local trust, local knowledge, and local rhythms of life. If policymakers want to learn from them, they must resist the temptation to impose one-size-fits-all models and instead fund the conditions for flexibility.

Perhaps the deeper lesson of community-level work is that digital equity is not purely about the relationship between the state and the individual. It is about the spaces in between—the meso-level of community, where human relationships can transform access into genuine agency. Libraries, NGOs, and centres embody a philosophy of equity that national device programmes often miss: that people need *places*, *mentors*, and *networks* as much as they need hardware. They show us that equity is built not only with money and machines but also with trust, patience, and imagination.

As the digital divide evolves, with inequalities now expressed as much in the depth of literacy as in basic access, the importance of these community institutions will only grow. They are not substitutes for systemic reform, but they are laboratories of possibility—places where society experiments with how to make digital learning meaningful in everyday lives. They reveal that equity is neither abstract nor theoretical but grounded in the question: *who is there to guide you when the screen lights up?* And the answer, far more often than national policy documents admit, is found in the quiet work of librarians, local volunteers, and community mentors who are holding open the digital door for those who might otherwise remain locked out.

The Role of Peer Mentorship

In contexts where formal digital education is underfunded, inaccessible, or misaligned with learners' realities, it is often peers rather than teachers who become the catalysts for genuine digital fluency. A striking insight emerges from classrooms, youth clubs, and community hubs across the world: *the most effective mentors are not always those furthest ahead, but those just one step further along.* Peer mentorship operates on this principle of proximity—of shared struggle and incremental mastery—and in doing so, it reshapes how digital skills are taught, shared, and absorbed in low-resource environments.

The misconception that technological competence must flow from experts to novices has long dominated both policy and pedagogy. Yet, in practice, the distribution of digital knowledge is rarely hierarchical. A teenager in a remote village may not have formal instruction in coding or data literacy, but they may be adept at navigating social media interfaces, troubleshooting mobile phones, or customising apps. When such a student shares their know-how with peers, they perform a crucial act of democratisation: they redistribute digital capital without the need for costly infrastructure or external intervention. In settings where professional trainers are scarce, *peer-to-peer knowledge sharing converts scarcity into an asset, turning everyday interactions into sites of education.*

Case studies from across the Global South illustrate the potency of this model. In Brazil's favelas, youth-led coding clubs have sprung up with minimal institutional support, often facilitated by young adults who only recently learned to programme themselves. Their relatability makes them effective mentors: they know the linguistic shortcuts, cultural references, and practical constraints of their peers. In India, the Digital Empowerment Foundation has documented how adolescent girls trained in basic ICT skills become "barefoot teachers" in their villages, teaching neighbours and siblings how to operate devices, use WhatsApp responsibly, and access government services online. The transmission is not merely technical; it carries with it an affirmation that learning is possible even in the absence of elite institutions.

One of the distinctive strengths of peer mentorship lies in its capacity to create learning environments free from the intimidation that often accompanies formal education. In hierarchical settings, students may fear asking "stupid" questions or admitting confusion, particularly in classrooms where teachers are overwhelmed or unfamiliar with the technologies themselves. Peers, by contrast, offer spaces of trust. A student might feel embarrassed to ask a teacher how to save a file, but they will readily seek help from a friend sitting beside them. Such dynamics are particularly crucial for marginalised learners, including girls in patriarchal societies or students with disabilities, for whom peer-led groups often serve as safe zones for exploration and growth.

There are, of course, tensions embedded within this model. Critics worry that peer mentorship risks reinforcing misinformation or superficial learning. After all, peers may lack the depth of understanding to correct misconceptions or introduce foundational concepts. A teenager may show a friend how to use a search engine but lack the critical literacy to explain why evaluating sources is necessary. Yet these concerns are not arguments against peer mentorship itself, but reminders of the need for supportive scaffolding. The most successful initiatives do not rely on peer mentors in isolation; they integrate them into broader networks of guidance, resources, and reflection. In this way, the peer mentor acts as a bridge rather than a substitute—making knowledge approachable while connecting learners to deeper reservoirs of expertise when needed.

What makes peer mentorship especially relevant in the digital age is its adaptability. Digital tools evolve so rapidly that even trained teachers may lag behind in their knowledge. Peer groups, by contrast, can adapt at the speed of platforms. When a new app emerges, it is often young users—not formal educators—who first explore its affordances, risks, and creative potentials. In refugee camps in Jordan, for example, adolescents have taught one another how to use mobile learning applications designed to support language acquisition and vocational training. Here, peer mentorship is not a stopgap measure but a dynamic process that keeps learning alive in fluid and unstable contexts.

Peer mentorship also has a profound social dimension. Unlike individualised digital learning models, peer-to-peer approaches weave digital competence into the fabric of community. Learning becomes communal, iterative, and reciprocal. A student who once received help in creating an email account may later guide another through online banking or digital safety practices. This reciprocity reinforces solidarity, undermining the competitive logics that often dominate education systems. *The act of teaching others consolidates one's own skills, turning learners into teachers and perpetuating cycles of empowerment.*

The impact extends beyond immediate skill acquisition. Peer mentorship nurtures confidence and agency. A young person who discovers they can teach others realises that they are not passive recipients of knowledge but active contributors to their community's digital resilience. In South Africa, township-based digital clubs have demonstrated this effect vividly: students who began by leading small tutorials on mobile phone use later became community advocates, pushing for better connectivity and infrastructure in their areas. The peer-mentor model thus generates not only digital fluency but civic engagement, intertwining technical and social empowerment.

Nonetheless, sustainability remains a challenge. Many peer mentorship projects are fragile, dependent on volunteer energy or short-term NGO initiatives. Without structural support—access to up-to-date devices, safe physical spaces for gathering, or modest stipends for mentors—such efforts risk burnout or decline. Governments and donors often overlook these informal networks in favour of large-scale, standardised programmes that appear more measurable. Yet the metrics of impact in peer mentorship are subtle: they are written in the confidence of learners, the spread of grassroots knowledge, the gradual embedding of digital fluency into everyday social life. Recognising and supporting these forms of learning requires a shift in how success is conceived and measured.

Peer mentorship is not a panacea, but it challenges deeply held assumptions about how digital skills are acquired and who counts as a legitimate teacher. It exposes the limits of access-centred approaches that equate devices with learning. It underscores the point that *knowledge is most transformative when it circulates through relationships of trust and reciprocity, not merely through transactions between experts and novices.*

In low-resource settings, where the digital divide is widest, this principle is not a luxury but a necessity.

If digital equity is to be more than rhetoric, then peer mentorship must be recognised not as an informal add-on but as a core component of strategy. The communities that have learned to teach themselves—to turn every smartphone-savvy child, every first-time coder, every curious neighbour into a mentor—are showing the world what a democratised digital future could look like. They remind us that the great promise of technology lies not in the devices themselves but in the networks of people who, step by step and peer by peer, learn to wield them together.

A Framework for Real Digital Equity

It is easy to mistake equality for equity in digital education. Distributing laptops or tablets to every child may appear like a decisive victory, a simple solution to the digital divide. Yet the persistence of gaps in achievement, confidence, and opportunity after such interventions reveals a harder truth: *access alone does not produce equity*. Real digital equity is not achieved by standardising tools but by recognising the differentiated needs of learners, communities, and educators, and by designing systems that provide literacy, guidance, and support alongside hardware. The future of digital learning will be shaped not by the sheer number of devices in circulation but by how intelligently we structure the ecosystems in which they are used.

The first principle of such a framework is recognising digital literacy as a continuum rather than a binary state. Many initiatives treat literacy as a checkbox—students are considered "digitally literate" once they can operate a keyboard, navigate a browser, or open a learning platform. Yet literacy in its fuller sense involves the capacity to evaluate information critically, understand privacy risks, create content, and engage responsibly in digital spaces. A student who can use Google to find quick answers but cannot distinguish between credible and manipulative sources is not meaningfully literate. The same holds for a child adept at operating a social media platform but unaware of its psychological manipulations. *Equity requires equipping learners not only with the ability to consume digital content but also with the intellectual armour to interpret and challenge it.*

The second principle is that equity must extend beyond students to include the adults who guide them. Teachers are often the most overlooked actors in digital strategies. Devices may be distributed en masse, but without sustained investment in teacher training, the potential impact diminishes sharply. Many educators report feeling unprepared to integrate technology meaningfully into their pedagogy. In low-income schools, where professional development is rare, the problem is especially acute. A framework for real equity must therefore include *systemic support for educators—continuous training, communities of practice, and access to mentors who can help them adapt technology to local contexts.* If the adults leading classrooms lack fluency and confidence, devices risk becoming distractions rather than enablers of deeper learning.

Third, the framework must address the role of families and communities. Children do not use devices in isolation; their digital practices are shaped by the habits, anxieties, and literacies of those around them. A laptop in the hands of a child whose parents can model balanced, critical, and creative digital use is vastly different from the same laptop in a household where parents are digitally excluded, overworked, or fearful of technology. This does not mean expecting all parents to become digital experts. Rather, it highlights the need for community-level support structures: libraries running evening digital literacy workshops, NGOs offering intergenerational training programmes, and public campaigns that normalise guidance rather than surveillance. *When digital equity is framed as a shared responsibility across schools, homes, and civic spaces, interventions begin to reshape cultures of learning rather than merely distributing gadgets.*

Economic and infrastructural realities cannot be ignored. A device without reliable connectivity is little more than a status symbol. Yet too often, governments invest heavily in hardware procurement while underfunding internet infrastructure, especially in rural areas. A framework for equity must therefore be rooted in *infrastructure justice*: affordable broadband, robust public Wi-Fi, and mechanisms to prevent entire regions from being digitally abandoned. This also means designing policies that confront not only access gaps but also affordability traps. A low-income family may own a smartphone, but if data costs remain prohibitive, their digital inclusion is hollow. Equitable policy ensures that connectivity is treated not as a luxury but as a public good, integral to participation in education and society.

A further element involves resisting the seduction of short-term metrics. Too many digital education policies are guided by quantifiable but shallow indicators: the number of devices distributed, logins to a platform, or hours spent online. These measurements can produce the illusion of progress while obscuring deeper inequities. Real equity is less easily captured but far more consequential. Are students developing critical thinking? Are marginalised learners gaining confidence to navigate online systems? Are communities using digital tools to expand opportunity, creativity, and agency? *A meaningful framework privileges these qualitative markers of growth over simplistic statistics, recognising that digital learning is measured by transformation, not compliance.*

Equity also demands adaptability to cultural and linguistic contexts. A platform designed for urban, English-speaking students in the Global North may be irrelevant or alienating to rural learners in sub-Saharan Africa or Southeast Asia. When educational content assumes homogeneity, it implicitly privileges those already closest to dominant cultural norms.

Equity therefore requires localisation: software translated into indigenous languages, case studies reflecting local realities, and content aligned with cultural traditions rather than erasing them. In this respect, digital equity echoes broader struggles for decolonising education. *True equity insists that learners see themselves reflected in their tools, rather than being forced to navigate platforms designed with someone else's reality in mind.*

Sustainability is another cornerstone. One-off device rollouts or short-term literacy workshops cannot deliver enduring equity. Communities need structures that evolve with technological change. This means embedding digital equity into long-term funding models, ensuring that schools can maintain and update hardware, and creating pathways for students to transition from basic digital literacy to advanced, employable skills. Sustainability also involves ecological responsibility: the rapid obsolescence of devices and the mounting problem of e-waste disproportionately burden low-resource communities. A just framework considers the lifecycle of technology and its wider environmental footprint, recognising that *digital equity cannot be achieved at the cost of planetary inequity.*

Finally, a framework for real digital equity must be rooted in values. Technology is not neutral; it encodes assumptions about what counts as success, what behaviours are rewarded, and whose voices are amplified. If digital education is shaped primarily by corporate interests, it risks reproducing consumerist logics rather than cultivating critical citizens. Equity therefore requires a normative stance: one that prioritises inclusion, criticality, creativity, and human flourishing over mere efficiency. Governments, educators, and communities must ask not only how technology is used but also *why it is used, and to what ends.*

Together, these principles sketch an alternative vision. Digital equity is not about ensuring that every child has the same device, nor is it about maximising online hours. It is about constructing ecosystems that weave together access, literacy, and guidance; that empower not only students but also teachers, parents, and communities; that respect cultural contexts while preparing learners for a globalised world; and that measure success not by numbers but by transformation. This vision resists the quick political win of photo-ready device handouts and instead demands patience, nuance, and investment in human infrastructure.

The challenge is formidable, but so is the cost of neglect. Without such a framework, digital interventions will continue to produce surface-level equality while leaving structural inequities intact. With it, however, education systems can begin to deliver on the real promise of technology: not the replication of old inequalities in new forms, but the cultivation of inclusive, resilient, and empowered digital citizens. *Real digital equity is not a finish line reached by distributing devices; it is a horizon continually advanced by equipping people, communities, and institutions to thrive in a digital world.*

Chapter 10
Building Digital Fluency for the Future

The distinction between access and fluency is becoming the defining challenge of modern education. To hand a student a laptop or a smartphone is to provide access; to equip them with the capacity to use that device critically, creatively, and responsibly is to cultivate fluency. Yet many systems conflate the two, assuming that the mere act of being online translates into competence. In truth, digital fluency is not the by-product of exposure; it is the result of deliberate, structured learning that transforms young people from passive users into active participants in shaping the digital world. *The future will not reward those who merely know how to navigate platforms but those who can question, adapt, and build within them.*

The first step towards this transformation is shifting students from users to makers. Consumption dominates much of children's online time: watching videos, scrolling feeds, playing games designed by others. While such activities familiarise them with interfaces, they rarely empower them to understand the architecture behind those systems. The danger of this asymmetry is that an entire generation may grow up as skilled consumers but remain disempowered in relation to the design, governance, and ownership of digital tools. By contrast, even modest exposure to creation—designing a simple app, building a website, editing media—reshapes confidence. Students begin to see technology as something malleable, not fixed; as a space for invention, not just entertainment. *This shift from user to maker is not about producing universal coders but about democratising agency in a world increasingly governed by algorithms and software.*

Coding exemplifies this point. It is often framed narrowly as a pathway to lucrative careers in software engineering, but its broader value lies in its mental discipline. Learning to code teaches students to deconstruct problems, recognise patterns, and build step-by-step solutions. These are transferable skills, akin to mathematical reasoning or scientific inquiry, but with particular resonance in a world mediated by machines. A student who understands loops, conditionals, or debugging—even at a basic level—cultivates habits of persistence and systems thinking that are valuable well beyond programming. To position coding as a new literacy is not to argue that every child must become a developer but to affirm that *the capacity to think computationally is now as fundamental to civic participation as the ability to read or write.*

Yet fluency cannot be reduced to technical competence alone. It must also encompass the ethical and civic dimensions of digital life. The same tools that enable creativity can also amplify misinformation, surveillance, and harm. If students are not taught to navigate these dilemmas, they inherit a landscape where power is asymmetrical and accountability scarce. Digital citizenship education therefore demands more than rules about online safety; it requires cultivating critical awareness of privacy, platform manipulation, and the responsibilities of participation in digital communities. Students must grapple with questions of authorship, bias, and intellectual property, learning not only how to protect themselves but how to contribute responsibly. *Ethics is not an optional add-on to digital fluency—it is its moral core.*

Alongside technical and ethical competencies, human skills retain a central place. Empathy, creativity, and critical thinking cannot be automated, yet they are often devalued in educational models overly fixated on technical proficiency. The paradox of the digital age is that the more tasks machines can perform, the more indispensable these human capacities become. A fluent digital citizen is not just someone who can code an algorithm but someone who can anticipate its social consequences, collaborate across cultural divides, and imagine alternative possibilities. As artificial intelligence, automation, and data-driven systems expand their reach, *the ability to combine technical literacy with distinctly human insight will determine whose voices shape the future.*

The work of building digital fluency is therefore not a marginal or elective task but a central responsibility of education. It demands curricula that balance creation with critique, coding with ethics, and technical proficiency with enduring human skills. It requires policymakers to invest not only in devices but in teacher training, community partnerships, and pedagogies that embed digital fluency across subjects. It invites families and communities to see technology not as a babysitter or a threat but as a shared space of learning where guidance matters as much as access. Above all, it challenges us to reimagine equity not as equal exposure to devices but as equitable preparation for participation in a digital world.

The chapters that follow will unpack these dimensions in detail. They will show how moving students from users to makers empowers them with agency, how coding can be reframed as a literacy for all rather than a vocation for a few, how ethical responsibility must be at the heart of digital education, and why human capacities such as empathy and creativity remain the foundation upon which all technological skill must rest. Taken together, these themes outline a vision of digital fluency not as a narrow technical goal but as a holistic framework for preparing citizens who can navigate, shape, and question the technologies that will define their future. *Fluency, in this sense, is not a skillset to be checked off but a mindset to be cultivated—an evolving capacity to live wisely and fully in a digital world.*

From Users to Makers

Handing a child a device is often celebrated as a step toward empowerment, yet this gesture too easily masks a deeper imbalance: most young people are trained, implicitly and explicitly, to consume digital products rather than to shape them. They scroll, click, and play, but rarely build. The cultural narrative that equates access with mastery obscures the fact that the architecture of our digital world is created by a relatively small minority, while the majority participate passively within pre-designed ecosystems. *If students are to thrive in a society defined by digital infrastructure, they must learn to approach technology not as fixed environments to navigate but as malleable systems they can design, adapt, and interrogate.*

The contrast between user and maker is not merely semantic. It reflects two fundamentally different relationships with technology. A user accepts the rules of engagement imposed by platforms, often without visibility into how those rules were coded, whose interests they serve, or what trade-offs they demand. A maker, by contrast, develops an awareness of design choices, logic flows, and potential alternatives. This awareness generates agency—the recognition that digital systems are human constructs, open to modification and contestation. Without this perspective, students risk internalising the idea that platforms are natural or inevitable, when in fact they are the outcome of corporate strategies, cultural assumptions, and technical decisions.

Consider the rise of social media. The majority of adolescents interact with these platforms through liking, sharing, and commenting—behaviours designed to sustain engagement. Yet only a fraction are equipped to question the algorithms that shape what they see or to build alternatives that might privilege different values. In classrooms where students are taught even rudimentary coding or interface design, the conversation shifts dramatically. They begin to see why one feature encourages endless scrolling while another nudges collaboration, or how data can be collected, visualised, and repurposed for community benefit. The simple act of moving from consumer to creator reframes technology as a field of contestable design rather than a natural habitat. *This reframing matters because democratic participation in a digital society requires the ability not just to use tools but to imagine and construct alternatives.*

The economic stakes of this divide are equally profound. The global digital economy thrives on a small pool of skilled creators designing tools for billions of passive users. This asymmetry produces both wealth concentration and cultural homogenisation. When education limits students to basic digital navigation—word processing, online research, app usage—it prepares them for dependency rather than autonomy. By contrast, when students learn to build, they open pathways not only to employment but to cultural representation and civic influence. A rural student in India who learns to design an application tailored to local needs is not merely improving career prospects but actively shaping how technology serves a community often overlooked by multinational corporations.

Critics sometimes argue that not every student needs to learn how to build digital tools, just as not everyone needs to be an engineer or architect. This view underestimates the broader value of making. Exposure to digital creation is not about producing a universal class of professional coders; it is about cultivating a mindset. A student who builds a simple game or edits open-source software learns persistence through debugging, logic through sequencing, and collaboration through shared projects. These experiences nurture habits of problem-solving and experimentation that extend far beyond the technical domain. *The point is not to produce more software developers but to produce citizens who can think critically about systems, identify limitations, and propose alternatives.*

There is also a psychological dimension worth noting. Consumption often leaves young people feeling dependent, even powerless, particularly when they encounter the darker aspects of online life—surveillance, misinformation, or addictive design. Making, by contrast, fosters a sense of control and possibility. Studies have shown that students engaged in digital creation demonstrate higher levels of confidence and resilience, not because they master a specific language or platform, but because they internalise the principle that systems can be understood and changed. In an age where technology pervades every dimension of social and economic life, *such a disposition towards agency may be one of the most valuable outcomes of education.*

Examples of this shift can be seen in initiatives around the world. Programmes like Code Club in the United Kingdom or CoderDojo globally provide children with accessible, community-driven environments to experiment with digital creation. These are not elite academies training future engineers but grassroots efforts designed to demystify coding and design for ordinary students. In classrooms where students collaborate to build a website for a local project or design a digital story that reflects their cultural heritage, the lesson is as much about expression and identity as it is about technical competence. These small interventions signal a profound pedagogical shift: technology is not only something imported into the classroom but something that can emerge from the classroom.

This does not mean the transition is straightforward. Many educators lack the confidence or training to guide students through digital making. The dominance of packaged educational technologies—preloaded apps, adaptive learning platforms, test-preparation software—encourages schools to adopt plug-and-play solutions rather than invest in building creative capacity. There is also a risk of widening inequalities: wealthier schools and families often provide children with access to maker spaces, robotics clubs, or coding camps, while disadvantaged communities are left with devices designed primarily for consumption. Addressing this imbalance requires policy and curricular commitments that treat digital creation as a baseline entitlement rather than an extracurricular luxury.

The cultural consequences of empowering students as makers are significant. A generation trained only to consume risks reinforcing existing hierarchies of technological power, where a few companies dictate the terms of interaction for billions. A generation encouraged to make, however, opens possibilities for more diverse forms of innovation. They are more likely to create tools that reflect local contexts, address underrepresented needs, or challenge exploitative models. They are also more likely to see themselves not as data points in someone else's platform but as designers of their own environments. *In this sense, making is not simply a technical skill but a democratic imperative.*

The challenge, then, is to embed this ethos of creation within education in ways that are inclusive, sustainable, and meaningful. That does not require every child to master multiple programming languages, but it does demand an educational philosophy that recognises digital fluency as more than access. It requires schools to balance consumption with creation, to equip teachers with the tools and confidence to guide experimentation, and to value the outcomes of making not only in terms of technical skill but in terms of agency, identity, and civic participation.

When students are empowered to move from users to makers, they are no longer limited to navigating the digital world as it exists. They gain the ability to question its assumptions, to reimagine its design, and to contribute to its evolution. That capacity—to see technology as something provisional, malleable, and subject to collective authorship—is the true marker of digital fluency. And it is what will distinguish those prepared to shape the future from those confined to consuming it.

Coding as a New Literacy

To describe coding as a new literacy may sound overstated in a world where most people will never earn a living as programmers. Yet to limit coding to the realm of professional careers is to miss its broader significance. Coding, at its core, is not just about writing instructions for machines; it is about developing habits of thought that are indispensable for navigating complex systems. Just as the invention of writing transformed how societies stored knowledge and reasoned about the world, coding represents a new form of symbolic literacy—one that trains individuals to think algorithmically, break down problems, and construct solutions in structured yet imaginative ways. *The real case for coding lies not in employability but in cognitive empowerment.*

The value of coding as a literacy begins with decomposition, the ability to take large, unwieldy problems and split them into smaller, manageable parts. This skill is evident in every discipline, from engineering to medicine to social work. A doctor diagnosing a patient, for instance, must parse symptoms into possible causes, test hypotheses, and evaluate outcomes. Coding forces students to practise this systematically: to define inputs, predict outputs, and anticipate errors. When children learn to programme even a simple game, they are compelled to ask, "What must happen first? What depends on what? How can I test if my assumption is correct?" Such structured reasoning spills over into everyday life, enhancing decision-making, planning, and resilience in the face of complexity.

Equally significant is the emphasis coding places on iteration. Unlike many school subjects where answers are framed as right or wrong, coding teaches that most problems require cycles of trial, error, and refinement. A misplaced comma can crash a programme, but debugging is not failure; it is an exercise in persistence and pattern recognition. This nurtures a mindset that views mistakes as part of the process rather than as deficiencies. *In an educational culture too often driven by high-stakes testing and fear of error, coding reintroduces the value of experimentation, reminding students that progress is seldom linear but built through revision and adaptation.*

Another dimension where coding enriches literacy is abstraction. To code effectively is to generalise principles: to see that a loop structure controlling a character's movement in a game is no different in form from a financial model calculating monthly interest. This act of abstraction cultivates the ability to move between contexts, recognising structural similarities beneath surface differences. Such thinking is increasingly vital in a world awash with information, where discerning patterns across domains often matters more than mastering detail within one.

Critics sometimes argue that promoting coding universally risks reducing education to vocational training, preparing students for jobs they may never want or that may not exist in future. This concern misinterprets the educational purpose. The point is not to churn out armies of coders but to expose all students to the logics underpinning the systems they inhabit. Just as literacy in reading and writing is not justified because everyone will become an author, coding literacy is not necessary because everyone will become a developer. It is necessary because *digital systems now mediate communication, governance, economics, and culture.* Understanding their logics at even a basic level is as fundamental as being able to parse a written sentence.

Case studies illustrate the transformative potential of this mindset. In Estonia, one of the most digitally advanced societies in the world, coding is introduced to children as early as primary school, not as a specialised skill but as an element of civic education. The intent is to ensure that citizens can understand and question the technologies structuring their daily lives, from e-government systems to digital healthcare. In the United States, initiatives like "Girls Who Code" focus not simply on employment opportunities but on building confidence and problem-solving skills in populations historically excluded from technology creation. Across very different contexts, the rationale is consistent: coding fluency nurtures agency in environments increasingly governed by digital systems.

There is also an ethical argument for coding literacy. If citizens lack even basic understanding of how algorithms work, they are less equipped to challenge biases embedded in automated systems, from predictive policing tools to hiring algorithms. Education that neglects coding leaves future generations vulnerable to opaque technologies that shape their opportunities and freedoms. Conversely, when students grasp how systems are built, they are more likely to interrogate their fairness, to demand transparency, and to imagine alternatives. *Coding is not only a technical capacity but a form of civic literacy, enabling people to participate more fully in debates about how technology should serve society.*

The challenge is that coding, unlike reading or numeracy, can seem intimidating, cloaked in jargon and professional mystique. Educational approaches that treat coding as advanced mathematics or as preparation for elite jobs reinforce this perception. To democratise coding as a literacy, it must be presented not as a specialised discipline but as a language of thought accessible to all. Visual programming environments like Scratch illustrate this principle: by allowing children to drag and drop blocks to create sequences, they learn logic and structure without the barrier of syntax. Similarly, creative projects—designing animations, interactive stories, or simple apps—ground coding in contexts that feel meaningful rather than abstract. The literacy emerges not from memorising commands but from experiencing the satisfaction of building something functional and expressive.

Importantly, coding intersects with creativity rather than opposing it. Too often, technology education is framed as the domain of the logical while the arts are framed as the domain of the imaginative. Coding disrupts this false dichotomy. To programme an interactive story requires narrative design; to create a simulation requires imagination about possibilities; to build a game requires aesthetic decisions about style, rhythm, and player experience. Coding, then, is a medium where logic and creativity converge. *By framing coding as a form of creative expression, education can broaden participation and underscore that digital fluency is not about replacing human imagination but amplifying it.*

At the same time, educators must navigate tensions. There is a risk of fetishising coding, treating it as the single answer to digital preparedness, overshadowing other literacies like media critique, online ethics, or collaborative skills. There is also the danger of reproducing inequalities, where well-funded schools offer rich maker spaces and dedicated coding modules while under-resourced schools limit technology education to test-preparation software. A genuine literacy movement requires equitable distribution of opportunities, so that coding is not the privilege of a few but a shared foundation for all.

In practice, this means embedding coding within broader frameworks of digital fluency. Students should learn not only how to write a loop or conditional statement but why systems are designed as they are, what values they embed, and how they can be reshaped. Coding should be taught alongside critical discussions of data privacy, algorithmic bias, and digital citizenship. By doing so, schools can position coding not as an isolated technical skill but as part of a holistic preparation for life in a society mediated by software.

The argument for coding as a new literacy rests, then, on its role as a mental model. It teaches decomposition, iteration, abstraction, and persistence—skills transferrable far beyond the screen. It cultivates agency in a digital environment otherwise dominated by passive consumption. It encourages creativity by blending logic with imagination. And it underpins civic participation by equipping citizens to interrogate and shape the technologies that govern their lives. Just as print literacy expanded who could access and contribute to culture, coding literacy has the potential to democratise not only opportunity but imagination itself. The societies that embrace this vision will produce generations not limited to using tools handed down to them but capable of designing, critiquing, and reinventing the digital worlds they inherit.

Digital Citizenship and Ethics

Few aspects of modern education are as urgent yet underdeveloped as the teaching of digital responsibility. Young people today are growing up in environments where every action online—liking a post, sharing a meme, entering personal data—contributes to a digital footprint that may outlast them. Yet the majority receive little structured guidance on how to navigate these spaces responsibly. Schools often provide access to devices but neglect to equip students with the ethical compass needed to use them wisely. *Without digital ethics education, we risk raising generations highly skilled in operating technology but unprepared for its moral, social, and civic consequences.*

At the heart of digital citizenship lies the question of responsibility: what it means to participate in online communities not only as consumers of information but as contributors and decision-makers. A student who spreads misinformation, even unintentionally, is not merely "using" the internet but shaping the informational ecosystem that others depend upon. Similarly, an adolescent sharing a classmate's embarrassing photo without consent participates in a culture of normalised harm. The capacity to access and manipulate digital tools does not guarantee discernment in their use; that discernment must be cultivated deliberately.

Privacy provides one of the clearest illustrations of this gap. Children and adolescents are constantly encouraged—often subtly by platform design—to trade personal data for convenience, entertainment, or connection. Signing up for a free game, they may click "accept" without reading terms that grant companies sweeping rights over their information. What begins as harmless play can create habits of complacency in adulthood, where sensitive data about finances, health, and location are surrendered with little thought. *Teaching privacy as a core principle of digital citizenship is not about fostering paranoia but about embedding critical awareness of the power dynamics implicit in every digital exchange.*

Case studies underscore the consequences of neglect. The Cambridge Analytica scandal revealed how personal data harvested through seemingly innocuous apps could be weaponised to influence elections. Meanwhile, cyberbullying cases demonstrate how ethical vacuums in youth behaviour can escalate into psychological harm, even suicide. These are not fringe occurrences but emblematic of systemic blind spots in education: we have been quicker to place tablets in classrooms than to ensure students understand the responsibilities accompanying their use.

One of the challenges in teaching digital ethics is that it resists the simplicity of rules. Unlike traditional civics education, where guidelines might be codified into laws or customs, online environments evolve too quickly for static codes to suffice. What counts as acceptable behaviour on a social platform today may shift tomorrow. Algorithms recalibrate, norms mutate, and new spaces emerge. Therefore, digital citizenship education must focus less on prescriptive do's and don'ts and more on cultivating *ethical reasoning skills*: the ability to weigh consequences, empathise with others, and anticipate how actions ripple outward in digital networks.

A constructive approach integrates ethical engagement with practical learning. For example, rather than lecturing students about online privacy, educators might guide them through exercises that reveal how much data they inadvertently share. When students see how a simple photograph can expose their location or habits through metadata, the abstract concept of digital traceability becomes tangible. Similarly, simulated debates about controversial online behaviour—whether it is reposting violent content, using AI to generate deepfakes, or sharing unverified health advice—can provide safe spaces to practise ethical judgement.

Philosophically, the task of digital citizenship education raises a tension between individual freedom and collective responsibility. On one hand, the internet is celebrated as a domain of personal expression. On the other, the collective nature of online ecosystems means that personal actions rarely remain private or isolated. The freedom to post a harmful rumour, for example, directly undermines the freedom of another to live without harassment. Students must learn to navigate this interplay, recognising that digital ethics is not about suppressing self-expression but about situating it within the rights and dignity of others.

A further dimension often overlooked is the role of power and inequality in shaping digital citizenship. Ethical engagement online is not the same for everyone. A wealthy student with strong parental support may have the resources to recover from identity theft or online harassment, while a child from a low-income background may face more severe consequences. Similarly, cultural norms influence how responsibility is understood: what counts as acceptable humour in one context may constitute harassment in another. *Effective digital ethics education must therefore be sensitive to diversity, acknowledging that rules cannot be applied universally without context.*

There is also the issue of algorithmic influence. Today's students are not only interacting with other humans online but also with systems that curate their reality—

recommendation engines, search algorithms, automated moderation. When a student searches for information on climate change or social justice, what they see is not neutral but shaped by hidden processes optimised for engagement. Digital citizenship in this sense extends beyond personal responsibility to include *algorithmic literacy*: an awareness that what one encounters online is curated and that critical engagement requires questioning not only people's motives but also systems' designs.

Schools are uniquely positioned to address these complexities but must avoid superficial gestures. Too often, "digital citizenship week" or anti-bullying assemblies serve as tokenistic substitutes for sustained engagement. What is needed is a curriculum that integrates ethics into every dimension of digital learning. A coding class should include discussions of bias in algorithms. A research project should include training in source evaluation and the dangers of misinformation. Even literature classes can adapt, asking students to reflect on how digital platforms reframe narrative, identity, and community. In other words, digital ethics should not be siloed as a one-off topic but woven into the fabric of education.

Parents, too, play a critical role, but many feel underprepared. The rapid evolution of platforms often leaves adults trailing behind their children in knowledge of digital culture. This generational lag complicates guidance: how can a parent counsel responsibility on TikTok if they barely understand its dynamics? Here, co-learning models offer promise. By engaging in joint exploration of online spaces—asking children to explain the appeal of platforms, discussing risks together—families can model ethical reflection rather than surveillance. *Ethics, after all, is best taught through dialogue rather than policing.*

The stakes extend beyond individual safety to the health of democratic societies. Citizens who lack digital ethics are vulnerable to manipulation, polarisation, and disengagement. The capacity to evaluate information critically, to resist the lure of outrage-driven content, and to participate constructively in online discourse is now foundational to democracy itself. This is why digital citizenship education should not be viewed as an optional add-on but as a civic imperative. Just as public schools once embraced civics to prepare citizens for industrial democracy, so must they embrace digital ethics to prepare citizens for networked democracy.

To argue for the centrality of digital citizenship and ethics is not to suggest that students must be shielded from the internet's risks by constant adult oversight. Instead, it is to advocate for empowerment: giving young people the frameworks, tools, and confidence to navigate ethical complexity themselves. Ultimately, the goal is not compliance but conscience—the ability to act with integrity even when no one is watching, even when the platform encourages recklessness. *Digital citizenship education, then, is less about producing rule-followers than about cultivating thoughtful participants in a shared, fragile, and profoundly interconnected digital world.*

The Human Skills That Endure

The more powerful our machines become, the clearer it is that some human capacities cannot be outsourced. Artificial intelligence can calculate faster than any mind, sift through oceans of data, and mimic styles of writing or art with impressive fluency. Yet even as these capabilities expand, they reveal their limits: algorithms lack empathy, they struggle to generate true originality, and they cannot evaluate meaning with the discernment that emerges from lived human experience. *In a hyper-digital world, the qualities that endure are not those that compete with machines but those that complement them—skills of empathy, creativity, and critical thinking that define what it means to be human.*

The danger of overlooking these skills is not hypothetical. Education systems, seduced by the promise of measurable outcomes and technological efficiency, often prioritise technical proficiency while neglecting what is harder to quantify. Coding assessments can test whether a student has memorised syntax; they cannot easily measure whether that same student can imagine how code might be used to solve a human problem, or whether they can reflect on the ethical consequences of their solution. The result is a generation trained to interact fluently with machines but ill-prepared to interact responsibly with each other.

Empathy sits at the core of this challenge. In digital spaces, where anonymity and distance can strip communication of nuance, empathy becomes both more difficult and more necessary. The rise of cyberbullying, online harassment, and disinformation campaigns is not primarily a technological issue but an empathetic one: an inability to recognise or value the humanity of others behind screens. Teaching empathy in the digital age cannot be limited to abstract moralising; it requires structured opportunities for perspective-taking. Role-playing scenarios where students experience the consequences of online harm, or collaborative projects with peers across cultures, can cultivate the habit of imagining the world through others' eyes. *Machines can replicate language, but they cannot replicate compassion. That remains uniquely our responsibility.*

Creativity, too, acquires new urgency. It is tempting to assume that creativity is undermined by AI's capacity to generate images, compose music, or draft essays. Yet these outputs, for all their surface fluency, rely on patterns drawn from pre-existing data. They are recombinations, not revolutions. Human creativity is distinguished not by novelty alone but by its capacity to *break frames*, to defy conventions, and to reimagine problems from angles that have never been attempted. When Picasso distorted perspective or when James Joyce fractured language in *Ulysses*, they did not merely rearrange what existed—they invented new modes of seeing and telling. In classrooms, this means that fostering creativity must involve more than offering digital tools; it demands pedagogies that encourage risk-taking, experimentation, and the courage to diverge from the expected.

Critical thinking provides the third pillar, and in many ways the one that anchors the others. In a digital ecosystem where information is abundant but often unreliable, the ability to evaluate, question, and synthesise is indispensable. A student who learns to code without critical thinking may create efficient programmes that reinforce bias or amplify misinformation. A young person who consumes news without critical literacy may fall prey to conspiracy theories or manipulation. To think critically is to resist passivity—to interrogate the source, to ask who benefits, and to imagine alternatives. *It is not enough to know how to use a tool; one must know how to question the structures that built it.*

Real-world examples illustrate these principles vividly. Consider the COVID-19 pandemic, during which misinformation spread online at speeds rivaling the virus itself. The technical capacity to use platforms did not protect individuals from being misled; what mattered was the human skill of evaluating claims, empathising with vulnerable populations, and creatively problem-solving under unprecedented constraints. Similarly, in the workplace, automation has eliminated many routine tasks, but it has elevated the value of employees who can collaborate across cultures, resolve conflicts with sensitivity, and innovate solutions to unstructured problems. These are not ancillary skills—they are survival skills in an economy where machines handle the predictable and humans are left to navigate the unpredictable.

Philosophically, the persistence of these human skills raises a profound question: what do we want education to produce? If the goal is to train efficient workers who can interface seamlessly with machines, then perhaps technical literacy alone will suffice. But if the goal is to cultivate citizens capable of shaping a just and humane society, then empathy, creativity, and critical thinking must sit at the centre. These are not luxuries; they are the foundations of civic life. A democracy cannot function if its citizens cannot imagine each other's needs, question authority, or invent better futures.

The educational implications are far-reaching. Classrooms that reduce learning to testable knowledge risk hollowing out the very qualities most needed in a digital age. Standardised exams may capture computational ability but rarely capture the ingenuity of a student who asks a disruptive question. Rubrics may reward formulaic essays but often penalise the risk of unconventional expression. To nurture enduring human skills, assessment itself must evolve—valuing process as much as product, dialogue as much as recall, and originality as much as correctness.

It is also essential to recognise that these human skills are mutually reinforcing rather than discrete. Empathy without critical thinking risks sentimentality; critical thinking without empathy risks cynicism; creativity without either risks irrelevance. When combined, however, they create the possibility of meaningful innovation—solutions that are imaginative, rigorous, and socially responsible. For example, designing an app to support mental health requires creativity in interface design, critical thinking in evaluating evidence-based practices, and empathy in understanding user experience. Strip away any one of these, and the result is either ineffective or harmful.

There are, of course, tensions and counterarguments. Some argue that empathy can be simulated, that AI companions designed for therapy or customer service may one day outperform humans in conveying care. Yet even if machines can mimic the appearance of empathy, the distinction lies in intention. Human empathy arises from vulnerability, from the recognition that we too can be harmed, that our dignity is intertwined with others'. A machine cannot *feel* in this sense; it can only model the outputs of feeling. Similarly, while generative AI can produce images that surprise us, it cannot hold the existential restlessness that drives human creativity—the dissatisfaction with what is and the longing for what might be.

If the digital future magnifies the importance of these skills, it also exposes how unequally they are cultivated. Privileged students, whose schools emphasise project-based learning, arts, and debate, may emerge with stronger capacities for empathy, creativity, and critical thinking than their peers in underfunded systems constrained by rigid testing. This inequity risks reinforcing not only economic divides but also civic divides, producing citizens unequally prepared to exercise judgement in a networked democracy. *Digital equity, therefore, must be understood not only as access to devices but as access to the cultivation of distinctly human capacities.*

Ultimately, the paradox of technological progress is that the more we automate, the more we must humanise. Machines excel at efficiency, but they are indifferent to meaning. Education, therefore, cannot content itself with teaching students to compete with machines on the machines' terms. Its task is to ensure that, in a hyper-digital world, the qualities that endure—empathy, creativity, and critical thinking—are not treated as peripheral "soft skills" but as the very essence of human intelligence. Only then will the next generation not merely survive the digital age but shape it in ways worthy of the name human.

Chapter 11
A New Model of Learning Equity

For decades, the central ambition of digital education policy has been simple: get devices into the hands of as many students as possible. The image of a child holding a school-issued laptop became an emblem of progress, a shorthand for closing the "digital divide." Yet the illusion of equality created by distribution has proved fragile. Access alone does not guarantee agency. A classroom of children with identical tablets may still contain profound inequalities—between those who can navigate, create, and question, and those who are confined to shallow forms of use. *The future of digital equity cannot be measured in the mere possession of hardware; it must be measured in the cultivation of agency—the ability to act, adapt, and discern in a complex digital world.*

This shift in perspective is more than semantic. It forces us to interrogate the assumptions that have guided reform and to confront the uncomfortable truth that devices, when distributed without guidance or support, can magnify rather than mitigate inequality. The wealthier child, whose parent can help decode unfamiliar interfaces or install beneficial learning apps, will turn a tablet into a portal of exploration. The less supported child may use the same device almost exclusively for entertainment, leaving their "access" functionally hollow. The metrics that policymakers celebrate—numbers of devices distributed, percentages of homes connected—fail to capture these subtler forms of inequity. If equity is to mean anything beyond numbers, it must be tied to the distribution of digital confidence, discernment, and opportunity.

To understand why agency matters more than access, consider the parallel of literacy. It is one thing to give every child a book; it is another to ensure that each child can read, comprehend, and think critically about its contents. Without literacy, access to a library is meaningless. The same holds for digital learning: the mere presence of a laptop does not cultivate the interpretive and evaluative skills that transform it into a genuine learning tool. This is where the old models of digital equity break down. They treat devices as an end, when in truth they are only a means.

Redesigning classrooms with this principle in mind demands more than adding screens or Wi-Fi. It requires a deliberate hybrid model, one that integrates the strengths of digital and analogue tools to support different forms of learning. A well-designed classroom might use digital platforms for collaborative writing projects while relying on face-to-face discussions to hone argumentation and empathy. A student might practise coding on a laptop in the morning and spend the afternoon prototyping their ideas with pen, paper, or physical materials. *Equity lies not in homogenising tools but in diversifying pathways—ensuring that each learner, regardless of background, encounters multiple avenues to agency.*

This hybridity also demands a rebalancing of responsibility. Too often, the burden of making technology meaningful is placed solely on teachers, who are expected to integrate new platforms into their curricula with minimal training, or on parents, who are asked to monitor usage without adequate digital literacy themselves. But learning equity cannot be constructed on the back of overextended teachers or parents. Instead, it requires collaborative models that connect the two spheres. Imagine a system where schools host regular workshops for parents on digital literacy, equipping them to understand the platforms their children use and to engage in guidance rather than surveillance. Picture teachers who are given time, support, and professional development not only to learn the mechanics of digital tools but also to critically evaluate their pedagogical worth. *When teachers and parents share the responsibility for cultivating digital agency, children experience coherence rather than contradiction between home and school.*

Real-world experiments point to what is possible. In Finland, for example, parents are invited into classrooms to learn alongside their children in certain digital literacy modules, creating a culture of shared discovery rather than generational division. In Singapore, teacher professional development includes explicit modules on the ethical, psychological, and creative dimensions of digital education—not just technical proficiency. These examples illustrate that equity emerges not from treating access as a box-ticking exercise but from embedding a broader ecosystem of support.

The true benchmark of equity, then, is not whether a child has a device but whether they can use that device to exercise judgement, creativity, and autonomy. It is not whether a student can log into a platform, but whether they can distinguish between misinformation and evidence, whether they can collaborate across cultural lines, whether they can move from consumer to creator. These are not "extra" skills; they are the new foundations of democratic participation and economic resilience. To measure equity without them is to mistake the means for the end.

There is a philosophical weight to this reframing. To prioritise agency over access is to assert that education is not a delivery system for content but a process of empowerment. It is to refuse the reduction of students to passive recipients of technology and instead to recognise them as active participants in shaping their digital futures. *An equitable system is not one in which every child has the same device, but one in which every child has the same capacity to shape their world through digital tools, guided by discernment, responsibility, and imagination.*

This chapter builds on the argument that has threaded throughout the book: that equity in the digital age is inseparable from literacy, guidance, and community. Here, we synthesise those insights into a new model—one that places agency at the centre, reimagines classrooms for hybridity, empowers teachers and parents as co-educators, and proposes agency itself as the measure of success. The challenge is not merely to bridge the gaps of today but to design a framework resilient enough for the uncertainties of tomorrow. If equity is to be meaningful, it must evolve beyond devices and infrastructure to encompass the deeper, harder, and ultimately more enduring task of cultivating human agency in a digital world.

Shifting the Lens from Access to Agency

The story of digital equity has long been told in numbers: how many households have broadband, how many classrooms are equipped with laptops, how many children are given a tablet on their first day of school. These statistics offer a convenient shorthand for progress, but they conceal more than they reveal. For beneath the surface of device counts and connection rates lies a deeper and more pressing question: what are learners actually able to *do* with the digital tools at their disposal? The central insight of our time is that access alone does not translate into empowerment. *True digital equity is not the equal distribution of devices, but the equal distribution of digital agency—the skills, confidence, and discernment that allow individuals to act meaningfully in a digital world.*

This reframing requires us to interrogate the complacency that comes with access-based metrics. A school district that proudly announces that every pupil now has a laptop may believe it has solved the digital divide, yet the reality on the ground often looks quite different. One child may use their laptop to code, create media, or collaborate on research projects, while another may be limited to repetitive drills or passive video consumption. Both children are "connected," but only one is building the habits of agency. This is the hidden fault line of twenty-first century education: not the divide between those with and without devices, but between those who use devices as platforms for agency and those who remain mere consumers.

Agency, in this context, is not a vague ideal. It encompasses a cluster of tangible capacities: the ability to evaluate information critically, to use tools for creative problem-solving, to navigate risks such as misinformation or exploitation, and to adapt to new technologies as they emerge. Agency also implies a degree of autonomy—the confidence to choose how to engage with digital systems rather than being passively shaped by them. Without this, the promise of digital equity collapses into hollow symbolism. We may create the outward appearance of equality while entrenching deeper forms of inequality, ones that are harder to see yet harder still to undo.

Consider the case of two secondary schools in the same city, both beneficiaries of an identical "one device per child" initiative. In the first, teachers are supported with training that enables them to integrate technology into project-based learning. Students design multimedia campaigns on climate change, simulate historical debates through online platforms, and collaborate with peers in other countries. The digital tool becomes a gateway to intellectual expansion and civic engagement. In the second school, teachers receive no training beyond basic technical support. Laptops are distributed, but lessons remain largely unchanged; students are instructed to copy notes from digital slides or fill in multiple-choice exercises online. The contrast is stark: identical devices, profoundly different outcomes. What separates the two schools is not access, but agency.

This distinction matters at the policy level as well. Governments and NGOs often prioritise access because it is easier to measure. Numbers of devices purchased, broadband subscriptions activated, and schools wired for connectivity can be readily tabulated, mapped, and publicised. Agency, by contrast, resists easy quantification. It develops unevenly, through a mix of pedagogy, mentorship, home environment, and peer culture. Yet this difficulty of measurement should not deter us. If anything, it underscores the need to invest in more nuanced metrics that capture how learners are using digital tools to advance skills, confidence, and critical literacy. Without this shift, we risk designing policies that deliver inputs but neglect outcomes.

One of the dangers of focusing on access is that it obscures the ways in which inequality is reproduced through digital systems themselves. A well-resourced child with supportive parents and access to extracurricular programmes may use their laptop to enrol in online courses, explore creative software, or engage in forums that enhance their learning. A less supported child, even with the same device, may default to algorithmically driven entertainment platforms designed to maximise engagement rather than learning. Here, equity is not a question of ownership but of orientation. The same tool becomes either a ladder or a trap, depending on the scaffolding provided. *This is why digital equity cannot be reduced to distribution; it must be about the cultivation of agency.*

The idea of agency also reframes how we think about the role of teachers. For too long, teachers have been positioned as gatekeepers of access—tasked with ensuring that students log on, complete assignments, and use devices responsibly. But if the goal is agency, teachers become facilitators of exploration, guiding students to harness digital tools in ways that promote independence and creativity. This shift requires professional development that goes beyond technical training to encompass pedagogical strategies for fostering agency. It means equipping teachers not only to manage devices but to mentor students in the habits of discernment, resilience, and ethical engagement.

Parents, too, play a critical role in the ecology of agency. Monitoring screen time, while useful, is insufficient. What matters more is helping children develop the confidence to ask questions about what they see online, to reflect on how technology influences their behaviour, and to make informed choices about their digital lives. In families where parents lack digital literacy, the absence of this guidance leaves children more vulnerable to exploitation or shallow engagement. Thus, equity is inseparable from parental involvement and from community-based support structures that can supplement gaps in the home.

Globally, some of the most promising models of digital equity already embody this emphasis on agency. Programmes that blend device provision with digital literacy training, peer mentorship, and teacher support consistently outperform access-only initiatives. In Kenya, for instance, community-based digital hubs combine access with workshops on critical thinking and entrepreneurial skills, ensuring that devices serve as catalysts for opportunity rather than distractions. In Canada, libraries have pioneered initiatives that integrate coding clubs and digital storytelling projects alongside traditional access programmes, transforming the library into a site of agency rather than mere connectivity. These examples demonstrate that when we expand our lens, equity becomes not just a distributional goal but a developmental one.

There is also a philosophical dimension to this reframing. To prioritise agency is to reaffirm the purpose of education itself: not simply to transmit information, but to cultivate the capacity to act wisely in an unpredictable world. In a digital age defined by rapid technological shifts, what matters most is not what devices we place in students' hands today, but whether they are prepared to navigate and shape the technologies of tomorrow. *Equity measured by access looks backwards—did we provide? Equity measured by agency looks forwards—can they thrive?*

By shifting the lens from access to agency, we begin to see digital equity not as a logistical challenge of distribution but as a moral and pedagogical imperative. It is about ensuring that every child, regardless of background, has the ability to harness technology for creation, communication, and critical thought. It is about dismantling the assumption that identical devices yield identical opportunities. And it is about recognising that the real measure of success lies not in what we give students, but in what they are able to do once they have it.

Designing Classrooms for the Hybrid Future

For more than a century, classrooms have been defined by the physical: desks arranged in rows, blackboards or whiteboards at the front, books and paper as the primary media of instruction. The digital revolution has disrupted this arrangement, but not yet replaced it. Instead, we find ourselves at a crossroads where education must reconcile the best of the analog past with the opportunities of the digital present. The challenge—and the promise—of the hybrid classroom is to integrate these worlds in ways that are not merely additive but transformative. The question is not whether schools should be digital or traditional, but how they can become environments where both modes work together to maximise learning for diverse groups of students.

One of the critical insights emerging from research on learning design is that digital and analog tools serve different, often complementary, purposes. Paper and pen are uniquely suited for deep processing of information: studies in cognitive science show that handwriting supports memory retention and conceptual understanding in ways that typing does not. At the same time, digital platforms excel at providing immediate feedback, enabling collaboration across distances, and giving students access to resources beyond their local environment. *The most effective classrooms of the future will not privilege one over the other but orchestrate their interplay, ensuring that students experience the full spectrum of learning modes.* A student might draft ideas by hand to stimulate conceptual thinking, then transfer them into a collaborative online document where peers and teachers can provide feedback in real time. Neither analogue nor digital is sufficient alone; the value lies in how they intersect.

Equally important is recognising that hybrid classrooms must account for the diversity of learners. Some students thrive in tactile, hands-on activities where the physical manipulation of materials cements understanding. Others are energised by the immediacy of digital interaction or the visual richness of multimedia resources. Designing for hybridity requires acknowledging this heterogeneity and creating flexible environments that do not force all learners into a single mode. For example, in mathematics instruction, one group of students might benefit from sketching geometric figures on paper, while another uses dynamic geometry software to explore transformations interactively. Both approaches lead to understanding, but the pathway differs. A truly equitable hybrid classroom treats this flexibility not as an indulgence but as a necessity.

The physical design of classrooms must evolve accordingly. Rows of desks facing a teacher no longer make sense in an age where knowledge flows multi-directionally and collaboration is central. Hybrid classrooms should be organised into zones: spaces where students can engage in quiet, analogue work; hubs for digital collaboration; and areas designed for group discussion and problem-solving. Schools that have piloted such models often report that student engagement increases not because of the technology itself, but because of the *choice* it affords. By allowing learners to shift between analogue and digital modes depending on the task, these classrooms embody the very agency that digital equity aspires to cultivate.

But hybridity is not just about the tools or spaces; it is about pedagogy. Teachers are central to making hybrid classrooms work, and this requires moving beyond the binary of "traditionalist" versus "tech enthusiast." Effective teachers in hybrid environments are those who understand the affordances and limitations of each mode and deploy them strategically. For example, a history teacher might begin with a traditional discussion of primary source documents, using physical reproductions that students annotate by hand. The discussion could then transition into a digital simulation where students model historical scenarios, followed by reflective essays that synthesise both experiences. Here, analogues ground the learning in detail and attentiveness, while digital tools expand the scope and immediacy of engagement.

This hybrid integration is particularly crucial for addressing inequities in learning outcomes. Research consistently shows that technology tends to amplify existing disparities: students who already have strong support and digital skills benefit disproportionately, while others are left behind. By embedding analog practices—such as structured note-taking, face-to-face dialogue, or physical experimentation—teachers can provide a stabilising framework that anchors students who might otherwise struggle in purely digital environments. Conversely, digital tools can provide scaffolding for students who find analogue methods limiting, such as those with dyslexia who benefit from text-to-speech software or those who require translation tools to access content. Hybrid design, when done well, is not just a compromise between old and new but a powerful strategy for inclusion.

The hybrid future also demands a rethinking of assessment. Traditional exams emphasise recall and individual work, whereas digital tools enable collaborative projects and iterative problem-solving. In hybrid classrooms, both forms of assessment must coexist. Students should demonstrate their ability to process information deeply in individual, analogue settings, while also showing their capacity to collaborate, adapt, and create in digital ones. This dual approach reflects the realities of the modern workplace, where professionals must often move seamlessly between solitary analysis and networked collaboration.

There is also a philosophical dimension to hybrid learning that is too often overlooked. By combining analogue and digital, classrooms remind us that learning is not about the fetishisation of tools but about cultivating habits of mind. Writing by hand slows thought, encouraging reflection. Online collaboration accelerates feedback, fostering adaptability. Discussion in person cultivates empathy and attentiveness, while digital platforms expose learners to diversity of thought on a global scale. *The hybrid model recognises that human flourishing in the digital age requires both the depth of analogue and the breadth of digital, both the slow work of contemplation and the fast work of connection.*

Examples of hybrid classrooms around the world illustrate how this integration can be realised. In Finland, primary schools often combine outdoor, hands-on activities with digital reflection journals, ensuring that physical experiences are connected to cognitive processing. In Singapore, mathematics classrooms integrate traditional problem-solving with adaptive digital platforms that personalise practice, freeing teachers to focus on higher-order discussion. In the United States, some schools have experimented with "maker spaces" adjacent to classrooms, where students move between constructing physical prototypes and modelling designs digitally. These approaches embody the spirit of hybridity: not replacement, but enrichment.

The transition to hybrid models will not be seamless. It requires investment not only in infrastructure but in teacher training, curriculum redesign, and cultural change. Teachers must feel confident navigating between modes, and students must be guided to see the value in both. The danger is that without deliberate design, hybrid classrooms devolve into chaotic mixtures where technology is bolted onto traditional methods without coherence. *The task is not to sprinkle digital tools into analog routines but to choreograph an interplay that is purposeful, equitable, and transformative.*

Ultimately, designing classrooms for the hybrid future is about preparing students for a world that will demand fluency across modes. The professional of tomorrow will draft ideas on paper, refine them on a digital platform, present them through multimedia, and defend them in face-to-face dialogue. Schools that prepare students only in one mode will leave them unprepared for the multiplicity of contexts they will encounter. By embracing hybridity, education can move beyond the false dichotomy of old versus new, creating classrooms that are not tethered to the past or enslaved to the future but oriented towards the full range of human learning.

The hybrid future, then, is not a transitional phase but a destination. It recognises that the tools of yesterday and tomorrow each have enduring roles to play, and that the real art of education lies in weaving them together. In this integration lies the possibility of a learning environment that is not only more effective but more humane—one that honours the cognitive, emotional, and social dimensions of learning by giving students the flexibility to engage in ways that are most meaningful to them. Designing such classrooms is not easy, but it is essential, for it is here that digital equity becomes tangible: not in the promise of access alone, but in the lived experience of agency and adaptability that hybrid learning makes possible.

… Teachers and Parents Together

… school have long existed as two parallel … education. Teachers are charged with …essment, parents with nurturing and … as digital learning environments increasingly blur the boundaries between classroom and household, this division appears increasingly inadequate. Children's experiences with technology are not confined to a school timetable, nor are they neatly separated from family life. Instead, learning is continuous, shaped as much by what happens in bedrooms, kitchens, and community spaces as by what unfolds within classroom walls. This reality demands new models of partnership—ones that recognise parents and teachers not as distinct actors performing separate roles, but as collaborators in cultivating digital agency and critical literacy.

The persistent problem is that many education systems continue to treat parents as peripheral: expected to ensure attendance, sign homework diaries, and enforce discipline, but rarely invited into the pedagogical conversation. In digital contexts, this marginalisation creates particular risks. A teacher may introduce a coding project in school, but if parents lack confidence with the same tools, they may default to disengagement, reinforcing inequalities. Similarly, when children encounter misinformation online or struggle with self-regulation around screen time, teachers alone cannot shoulder the burden of guidance. *To empower students, we must first empower the adults around them—parents and teachers together—to act as co-educators in the digital sphere.*

Collaboration between parents and teachers is not a romantic ideal but a practical necessity. Consider the rapid pivot to online learning during the COVID-19 pandemic: households across the globe became classrooms overnight, and parents, regardless of their digital literacy, found themselves supervising lessons. While this exposed deep inequities, it also revealed a truth often overlooked—that parents, when supported, can become powerful allies in education. Some schools responded by creating regular webinars for parents on digital tools, establishing helplines staffed by teachers, or pairing digitally skilled parents with those less confider
These experiments showed that when schools invite par

into the learning process, the benefits extend beyond crisis management. Families become more confident in supporting their children, and teachers gain valuable insights into how learning continues at home.

Yet genuine partnership requires moving beyond token gestures. Parent–teacher evenings, often rushed and perfunctory, cannot build the trust needed for collaboration. Instead, schools must design structures that make partnership ongoing, relational, and reciprocal. For instance, some schools have experimented with "digital literacy circles" where teachers, parents, and even students meet to share experiences of navigating the online world. In these settings, parents' practical knowledge of their children's digital habits complements teachers' expertise in pedagogy. Such initiatives do not merely transfer knowledge; they cultivate a shared vocabulary, enabling adults to offer consistent guidance across home and school contexts.

The challenge is particularly acute in low-income or marginalised communities, where digital divides intersect with cultural and linguistic barriers. Here, collaborative models must be both inclusive and culturally responsive. NGOs in countries such as India and Kenya have shown how parent–teacher partnerships can be fostered even where access is limited. By holding community workshops in local languages and involving parents in designing after-school digital programmes, they reduce the gap between the tools children use in school and the realities of their home environments. *The principle is clear: without intentional strategies to engage parents, especially those most excluded from digital literacy themselves, the promise of educational technology risks deepening rather than bridging divides.*

Teachers also benefit when collaboration is prioritised. Too often, the responsibility for mediating digital tools, addressing cyberbullying, or teaching online ethics falls squarely on their shoulders. This not only overburdens educators but narrows the effectiveness of interventions. When parents are equipped with complementary knowledge and confidence, responsibility is shared, and reinforcement happens across environments. For example, when a school introduces lessons on digital citizenship, parents who are briefed on the same themes can reinforce those lessons during conversations at home about online behaviour. The consistency between messages delivered in class and those echoed at the dinner table is what makes guidance stick.

However, building such coherence requires careful attention to power dynamics. Teachers, accustomed to being seen as the professionals, may hesitate to open their practice to parental scrutiny. Parents, conversely, may feel intimidated by education jargon or judged for their lack of digital competence. Successful models of collaboration address these tensions explicitly. One approach is to reframe engagement not as teachers instructing parents, but as mutual learning. Parents bring invaluable insights into children's behaviour, motivations, and struggles at home; teachers contribute expertise on curriculum and pedagogy. When both contributions are valued, collaboration becomes less hierarchical and more productive.

There is also an intergenerational aspect to this partnership. Many parents belong to a generation that encountered the digital world as adults, while their children are immersed from birth. This asymmetry can lead to feelings of inadequacy, fuelling withdrawal rather than engagement. Schools that acknowledge this divide and provide parents with opportunities to learn alongside their children create more sustainable models. Workshops where parents and students explore digital tools together, guided by teachers, not only build competence but model the kind of co-learning that strengthens family bonds. *By reducing the gap between adult hesitation and child enthusiasm, such initiatives transform technology from a source of tension into a shared space of discovery.*

Importantly, empowering parents and teachers together also means rethinking communication practices. Too often, school communication with families is transactional: report cards, reminders, warnings. In hybrid learning environments, where technology links classrooms to homes daily, communication can instead become dialogical. Apps and platforms that allow two-way interaction—where parents can share observations, ask questions, and access resources—shift the relationship from oversight to collaboration. For example, some schools now use messaging systems where teachers share weekly updates not only about grades but about the digital skills being developed, enabling parents to engage more meaningfully.

Critically, these models must avoid assuming that all parents have unlimited time or resources to engage. Many caregivers work multiple jobs, lack reliable internet, or face other pressures. Collaborative models must therefore be flexible: offering recordings of workshops rather than only live sessions, providing resources in multiple languages, and respecting diverse family circumstances. When engagement is framed as an obligation, it risks alienating those already struggling. When framed as an invitation, backed with practical support, it becomes empowering.

Policy, too, has a role in embedding these partnerships. Governments often fund devices or digital infrastructure but neglect the relational side of learning. By supporting initiatives that build parental capacity, governments can amplify the effectiveness of their investments. Imagine if every national digital literacy programme included a parent component, with funding for training and resources tailored to household realities. Such policies would recognise that *digital equity is not achieved by equipping students alone, but by enabling the adults around them to guide and sustain learning.*

The deeper philosophical point here is that learning in the digital age is not confined to institutions. Children oscillate constantly between home, school, and online spaces, carrying ideas, behaviours, and risks across these boundaries. Fragmented approaches—where teachers focus on curriculum and parents on discipline—cannot address this fluidity. Only when both sides act as partners, aligned in vision and practice, can children be equipped with the discernment and confidence needed for meaningful digital agency. The hybrid future of education will not be built solely on devices, platforms, or policies, but on relationships. And at the heart of those relationships must be a partnership between the adults who share responsibility for children's growth.

To empower teachers and parents together is not to dissolve their distinct roles but to weave them into complementarity. Teachers cannot know every nuance of a child's digital life, just as parents cannot replicate the expertise of educators. But when these insights meet, a more holistic picture emerges. The child is seen not only as a student or as a son or daughter, but as a learner whose growth spans multiple environments. This is the promise of collaboration: not a burden shared reluctantly, but a responsibility embraced collectively, rooted in the recognition that education in a digital world is simply too complex for any one actor to manage alone.

Agency as the True Measure of Success

For more than two decades, the rhetoric of digital equity has been dominated by a deceptively simple metric: the distribution of devices. If every student has a laptop or tablet, the thinking goes, the digital divide is solved. This narrative has been politically attractive because it lends itself to tangible action—numbers of devices purchased, networks installed, access points deployed. Yet the illusion of progress obscures a deeper truth: *equity is not achieved by distributing tools, but by cultivating the confidence, discernment, and agency to use them meaningfully*. A child who owns a device but cannot distinguish misinformation from fact, or who lacks the skills to transform information into knowledge, is no closer to opportunity than one who has no device at all.

The inadequacy of device-focused equity is evident in the outcomes of well-intentioned but shallow interventions. Consider the One Laptop per Child initiative, hailed as revolutionary when it launched in the mid-2000s. It succeeded in placing millions of devices into the hands of children across developing countries, yet multiple evaluations showed limited impact on literacy, numeracy, or higher-order thinking. The missing link was not access, but scaffolding. Without well-trained teachers, supportive parents, and culturally relevant content, the devices became underutilised or relegated to entertainment. *Hardware without human guidance breeds only surface-level familiarity, not genuine empowerment.*

This insight forces a reframing of what digital equity ought to mean. If equity is measured only by possession, the most vital dimensions of learning are ignored. True equity demands that every learner develops digital confidence—the sense that they can navigate unfamiliar tools without fear; discernment—the ability to question sources, detect manipulation, and make informed choices; and opportunity—the structural conditions that allow these capacities to translate into real social and economic participation. Access alone provides the canvas; agency fills it with meaning.

The importance of confidence cannot be overstated. In classrooms where children hesitate to experiment for fear of "breaking" the technology, the promise of learning stalls. Conversely, when children are encouraged to test, fail, and try again, they develop resilience and adaptability—the very traits required in a rapidly changing digital economy. Confidence is not innate; it emerges from guided practice, mentorship, and the presence of adults who model curiosity rather than intimidation in the face of technology. Schools that prioritise confidence-building activities—such as open-ended projects where outcomes are not predetermined—often produce learners who can transfer digital skills across contexts rather than merely reproducing narrow routines.

Discernment, too, is a skill rarely captured by conventional metrics. Education systems have tended to equate digital proficiency with technical ability: can a child code, search, or create a presentation? Yet these skills mean little without the intellectual muscle to evaluate what is being coded, searched, or presented. The proliferation of deepfakes, algorithmic bias, and targeted disinformation underscores that the greatest risks of the digital age are not technical barriers but epistemic ones. To be digitally literate is not simply to operate tools but to interrogate them. When a teenager encounters a news story on social media, equity is not whether they can read it on their own device, but whether they can weigh its credibility, recognise its framing, and situate it within a wider informational landscape.

Opportunity extends the conversation from individual capacity to structural context. A rural student who masters coding on a donated tablet but has no broadband access or local tech industry may find their skills underutilised. Similarly, a child from a disadvantaged urban neighbourhood may excel in digital creativity but lack pathways to showcase or monetise that work. Opportunity requires policies that address infrastructure, yes, but also mentorship networks, industry partnerships, and inclusive platforms for participation. It is the translation of skills into mobility—economic, social, and cultural—that defines whether equity has been achieved. *Without opportunity, confidence and discernment risk becoming talents that wither unused.*

This reframing also challenges how success in digital education is assessed. Many governments report progress in terms of student-device ratios, classroom connectivity, or hours of screen-based learning. Yet such measures are proxies, not outcomes. The real benchmark is whether learners emerge as agents—individuals who can adapt technologies to their goals, who can critique and resist harmful digital dynamics, and who can harness digital tools for creativity, collaboration, and problem-solving. This shift mirrors broader debates in education about moving from rote learning to competencies. Just as memorising facts does not guarantee understanding, distributing devices does not guarantee equity.

The shift from access to agency demands new pedagogical priorities. Teachers must be empowered to facilitate inquiry rather than deliver digital skills as checklists. Curricula must embed critical thinking about technology—how algorithms shape information flows, how data is commodified, how design reflects bias. Parents must be drawn into the process, not as enforcers of screen time but as co-learners who model ethical engagement. And policymakers must resist the temptation of headline-friendly interventions in favour of sustained investment in teacher training, community infrastructure, and evaluative frameworks that measure agency rather than inventory.

There are encouraging models that point the way. In Uruguay, the Plan Ceibal project began with device distribution but evolved into a holistic ecosystem: teacher development, online platforms, and nationwide initiatives that connected schools with cultural institutions. Its success was not in the laptops per se but in the capacity-building around them. In Finland, digital literacy is integrated across subjects, emphasising critical evaluation of online sources as much as technical competence. In both cases, the emphasis is on shaping citizens who can navigate digital society with autonomy and responsibility, not merely on provisioning hardware.

This approach also resonates with broader philosophical concerns about education. The aim of schooling has never been merely to provide access to knowledge, but to cultivate judgement in its use. In the digital age, that mission takes on renewed urgency. Agency is what allows students to transcend being passive recipients of information and instead become critical actors—capable of shaping their environments rather than being shaped by them. In this sense, digital equity is not only about fairness in education but about democracy itself. A society where only a fraction can meaningfully exercise digital agency risks deepening divisions of power and voice.

The reframing from access to agency does not dismiss the importance of infrastructure or devices—they remain prerequisites. But it refuses to stop there. The deeper challenge is cultural and pedagogical: equipping all learners not just to use technology, but to command it with confidence, critique, and creativity. Success, therefore, cannot be tallied in spreadsheets of distributed hardware. It must be seen in the eyes of students who question, experiment, and apply digital tools in ways that expand their horizons. When digital equity is measured by agency, not access, the goal is no longer to close the gap in ownership, but to open the field of opportunity.

About the Author

Rowan Hart writes at the intersection of education, technology, and social justice. Having worked alongside public schools, community nonprofits, and mission-driven startups, Rowan focuses on how tools shape learning only when guidance, culture, and equity are built in. Their reporting-driven approach blends classroom observation with accessible analysis, translating research into practical choices for teachers, parents, and policymakers. Rowan's work champions a simple idea: access to devices means little without the confidence, discernment, and support to use them well. When not interviewing educators or mapping learning ecosystems, Rowan mentors youth media projects and helps schools design low-lift, high-impact digital literacy practices.

www.ingramcontent.com/pod-product-compliance
Lightning Source LLC
Chambersburg PA
CBHW031341230926
51848CB00002B/336
9789371773003